鹏程: 中国新诗百年

New Poetry from China

1917–2017

edited by Ming Di

Introduced by John Yau

translated by Ming Di & Kerry Shawn Keys
with significant translations by
Gregory Pardlo, Kevin Young
Tracy K. Smith & others

BSE

ISBN: 978-0-9898103-8-8

BSE Books are distributed by
  Small Press Distribution
  1341 Seventh Street
  Berkeley, CA 94710
  orders@spdbooks.org | www.spdbooks.org | 1-800-869-7553

BSE Books can also be purchased at www.blacksquareeditions.org and www.hyperallergic.com

Contributions to BSE can be made to
  Off the Park Press, Inc.
  1156 Martine Ave.
  Plainfield, NJ 07060
  (Please make checks payable to Off the Park Press, Inc.)

To contact the Press please write:
  Black Square Editions
  1200 Broadway, Suite 3C
  New York, NY 10001

An independent subsidiary of Off the Park Press, Inc.

Member of CLMP.

Publisher: John Yau
Editors: Ronna Lebo and Boni Joi
Design & composition: Shanna Compton

Cover art: "Land of Small Gods" by Jike Bu, oil painting on canvas, 60 x 80 cm, 2014. By kind permission of the artist.

Contents

9 **INTRODUCTION** by John Yau

13 **FOREWORD** by Ming Di

 Journey of Peng: One Hundred Years of New Poetry
 in China　鵬程：中国新诗百年

19 **MAJOR EVENTS IN THE LAST ONE HUNDRED YEARS**　百年大事记

25 Hu Shi　胡适　(1891–1962)

28 Wen Yiduo　闻一多　(1899–1946)

30 Li Jinfa　李金发　(1900–1976)

32 Fei Ming　废名　(1901–1970)

34 Feng Zhi　冯至　(1905–1993)

36 Dai Wangshu　戴望舒　(1905–1950)

37 Bian Zhilin　卞之琳　(1910–2000)

38 Ji Xian　纪弦　(1913–2013)

40 Zhu Yingdan　朱英诞　(1913–1983)

42 Chen Jingrong　陈敬蓉　(1917–1989)

44 Mu Dan　穆旦　(1918–1977)

46 Zheng Min　郑敏　(1920–)

48 Wu Xinghua　吴兴华　(1921–1966)

49 Lü Yuan　绿原　(1922–2009)

50 Luo Fu　洛夫　(1928–2018)

51 Guan Guan　管管　(1929–)

52 Shang Qin　商禽　(1930–2010)

53 Zheng Chouyu　郑愁予　(1933–)

54 Chang Yao　昌耀　(1936–2000)

55 Huang Xiang　黄翔　(1941–)

56 Luo Qing　罗青　(1948–)

57 Bei Dao　北岛　(1949–)

59 Liang Bingjun　梁秉钧　(1949–2013)

61 Mang Ke　芒克　(1950–)

62 Duo Duo　多多　(1951–)

67 Gen Zi　根子　(1951–)

70 Yi Lei　伊蕾　（1951–2018）

72 Yan Li　严力　（1954–）

74 Yu Jian　于坚　（1954–）

77 Yang Lian　杨炼　（1955–）

79 Wang Xiaoni　王小妮　（1955–）

80 Zhai Yongming　翟永明　（1955–）

82 Mo Yan　莫言　（1955–）

84 Liu Xiaobo　刘晓波　（1955–2017）

86 Ouyang Jianghe　欧阳江河　（1956–）

88 Sun Wenbo　孙文波　（1956–）

90 Zhang Shuguang　张曙光　（1956–）

92 Bai Hua　柏桦　（1956–）

93 Tong Wei　童蔚　（1956–）

94 Wang Jiaxin　王家新　（1957–）

96 Liao Yiwu　廖亦武　（1958–）

98 Song Lin　宋琳　（1959–）

100 Xiao Kaiyu　萧开愚　（1960–）

102 Lü De'an　吕德安　（1960–）

105 Mo Fei　莫非　（1960–）

107 Han Dong　韩东　（1961–）

109 Chen Dongdong　陈东东　（1961–）

111 Jidi Majia　吉狄马加　（1961–）

113 Luo Yihe　骆一禾　（1961–1989）

114 Liu Xia　刘霞　（1961–）

116 Zhang Zao　张枣　（1962–2010）

117 Qing Ping　清平　（1962–）

119 Wang Yin　王寅　（1962–）

120 Sen Zi　森子　（1962–）

122 Xi Chuan　西川　（1963–）

125 Li Yawei　李亚伟　（1963–）

127 Li Yuansheng　李元胜　（1963–）

129 Yang Xiaobin　杨小滨　（1963–）

130 Zhang Qinghua　张清华　（1963–）

132 Zhou Qingrong　周庆荣　（1963–）

134 Pan Xichen 潘洗尘 （1963-）

136 Hai Zi 海子 （1964-1989）

138 Zang Di 臧棣 （1964-）

141 Song Wei 宋炜 （1964-）

144 Zhao Ye 赵野 （1964-）

145 Mo Mo 默默 （1964-）

147 Na Ye 娜夜 （1964-）

149 Pan Wei 潘维 （1964-）

151 Xiao Xiao 潇潇 （1964-）

152 Shen Wei 沈苇 （1965-）

154 Zhang Zhihao 张执浩 （1965-）

156 Shu Cai 树才 （1965-）

157 Yu Xiaozhong 余笑忠 （1965-）

159 Yi Sha 伊沙 （1966-）

160 Lei Pingyang 雷平阳 （1966-）

161 Gu Ma 古马 （1966-）

162 Li Sen 李森 （1966-）

164 Hu Xian 胡弦 （1966-）

165 Chi Lingyun 池凌云 （1966-）

166 Yu Nu 余怒 （1966-）

167 Xi Du 西渡 （1967-）

169 Chen Xianfa 陈先发 （1967-）

171 Sang Ke 桑克 （1967-）

173 Lan Lan 蓝蓝 （1967-）

174 Li Shaojun 李少君 （1967-）

175 Lin Zi 琳子 （1967-）

176 Jing Wendong 敬文东 （1968-）

177 Huang Bin 黄斌 （1968-）

178 Zhu Zhu 朱朱 （1969-）

179 Qiu Huadong 邱华栋 （1969-）

181 An Qi 安琪 （1969-）

182 Jiang Tao 姜涛 （1970-）

184 Yu Xiang 宇向 （1970-）

185 Ni Zhijuan　倪志娟　(1970–)

186 Xi Wa　西娃　(1970–)

188 Jiang Hao　蒋浩　(1971–)

191 Xuanyuan Shike　轩辕轼轲　(1971–)

193 Lü Yue　吕约　(1972–)

195 Han Bo　韩博　(1973–)

197 Leng Shuang　冷霜　(1973–)

198 Quan Zi　泉子　(1973–)

200 Chen Jun　陈均　(1974–)

202 Hu Xudong　胡续冬　(1974–)

204 Qin Xiaoyu　秦晓宇　(1974–)

206 Mu Cao　墓草　(1974–)

207 Shen Haobo　沈浩波　(1976–)

209 Yu Xiuhua　余秀华　(1976–)

211 Zhang Er　张尔　(1976–)

212 Jiang Li　江离　(1978–)

213 Li Hongwei　李宏伟　(1978–)

215 Ma Yan　马雁　(1979–2010)

216 Zheng Xiaoqiong　郑小琼　(1980–)

218 Xiao Shui　肖水　(1980–)

220 Yuan Yongping　袁永苹　(1983–)

221 Li Heng　黎衡　(1986–)

222 Jike Bu　吉克·布　(1986–)

224 Kawa Niangji　卡瓦娘吉　ལྭགས་ཀྱི་ཉིན་བྱེས།　(1989–2015)

226 Xu Lizhi　许立志　(1990–2014)

227 Qin Sanshu　秦三澍　(1991–)

229 Su Xiaoyan　苏笑嫣　(1992–)

233 **Afterword**
　　　From butterflies to living words, Rereading Hu Shi
　　　从蝴蝶到活文字: 重读胡适

251 **Acknowledgments**

Introduction

ONE OF THE MANY CHALLENGES a poet faces is the renovation of language. How do you defy the familiar patterns that language perpetually falls into, even in literature? While the renovation can take many forms, a recurring focus concerns the subject of common life and the use of the vernacular. From Catullus and Du Fu, we learn about ordinary life in ancient Rome and China. Their work opened up their respective languages and changed the poetry of their time, helping shape what came after. Countless generations of poets have hankered after the impassioned directness with which the lyric poems of Catullus and Du Fu wrestled with their tumultuous, emotionally fraught moment.

I suspect the motivation to overhaul language derives from the desire to break the tyranny of poetry's strict forms or approved subject matter. Inevitably, forms become stale, and accepted subjects devolve into clichés. The past is not something poets inherit, like a pair of old shoes they must try to fit into.

This anthology, *New Poetry from China 1917–2017*, begins with a section of a long poem in dialog, "Reply to Old Mei—A Poem in Plain Speech," written by Hu Shi (1891–1962) in 1916. As Ming Di, who painstakingly researched and assembled the anthology, states at the beginning of her essay on rereading Hu Shi: "It's hard to believe that what we call avant-garde poetry today started a hundred years ago."

Hu Shi's poem marks the beginning of free verse in China, which broke apart, in Ming Di's characterization, "three thousand years [. . .] of what's called 'classical poetry.'" His "Eight don'ts," which was published in the journal *New Youth* (Shanghai, 1916), shares something with T. E. Hulme's "A Lecture on Modern Poetry" (1908) and Ezra Pound's "A Few Don'ts by an Imagiste" (1913). In his warning against sentimentality and the use of clichés, as well as his championing of the use of slang and colloquial speech in poetry, Hu Shi is promoting free verse written in the vernacular.

Although there is no proof, it has been speculated that Hu Shi might have been influenced by what he read in *Poetry* magazine while a student at Columbia University. If true, Hu Shi would have read, in the March 1915 issue, Ezra Pound's translation of Li Po's poem, "Exile's Letter," into free verse, which eliminated the strict meter and rhyme scheme of Li Po's original. If this piqued Hu Shi's curiosity, he might have gone to a bookstore to find Pound's recently published *Cathay* (1915), which contained his translation of fifteen classical Chinese poems. Again, in *Cathay*, Hu Shi would have read poems that did not adhere to the original form and rhyme scheme. Pound had "translated" the poems from a language he could neither read nor speak, basing his work on notes and translations by the art historian Ernest Fenollosa, and arrived at something that not been seen before in English.

The publication of *Cathay* had a profound influence on Pound's peers and contemporaries. However, Pound did not write *Cathay* in a bubble, nor was Fenollosa his only influence. Part of his interest in condensed language and direct expression began in 1909, when he met T. E. Hulme, one of the founders of Imagism. I mention this because the renovation of language is almost always the result of various efforts by poets and translators.

New Poetry from China 1917–2017 is an initiative spearheaded by Ming Di that involves Chinese and American poets working together to translate more than 130 poems by more than one hundred poets born between 1891 and 1991. The United States Poet Laureate

Tracy K. Smith, the Pulitzer Prize-winning poet Gregory Pardlo, and the well-known poet, essayist, and current poetry editor of the *New Yorker*, Kevin Young, all contributed mightily to the making of this book.

In contrast to other anthologies of modern Chinese poetry, Ming Di includes ethnic and religious "minority" poets who are Tibetan, Manchu, Muslim, Mongolian, and Yi. She has represented China's ethnic diversity, publishing poets who live and work in very different geographic locales. In 2017, nearly eighty years after W. H. Auden traveled to Wuhan in 1938 and published *Journey to a War* with Christopher Isherwood, I traveled to Wuhan to meet Zhang Zhihao and other poets from central China. Ming Di, who was born in Wuhan and has lived in many places in this "Province of a Thousand Lakes," has presented us with the first translations ever made of poets from this and other parts of China, whether established or young and lesser-known, enriching our sense of Chinese poetry from the past one hundred years.

In this anthology, readers will find many memorable texts by poets they are likely never to have heard of before. They will get a taste of the modern poetry written in China during one of the most decisive epochs of its long, turbulent history—a century marked by war, revolution, and famine.

Poetry has long occupied a place of honor in China. It is not ignored or dismissed, as it so often is in America. The poets included in this anthology come from every part of a vast country, from the cities and the countryside. There are professors, journalists, farmers, laborers, and activists. There are straight poets and gay poets. There is a poem by Kawa Niangji, a Tibetan poet and environmental activist, and by Xu Lizhi, a migrant worker who worked for Foxconn, which produces most of the world's iPhones. He committed suicide at the age of twenty-four, leaving behind more than two hundred poems. There is a powerful and tender poem by Liu Xiaobo, who received a Nobel Peace Prize and died a political prisoner. There are poems by writers who are legendary figures in China, such as Mo Mo, who is hardly known elsewhere. And there are offerings by poets such as Duo Duo, Bei Dao, Zhai Yongming, and Ouyang Jianghe, whose books have been translated and published abroad, including the United States.

There is "Crossing Half of China to Sleep with You," an erotic political love poem by Yu Xiuhua, who is from central China's rural Hubei province and hates to be compared to Emily Dickinson or anyone else. There is nothing compliant about the poets or poems in this anthology.

In China, where writing poetry can be dangerous, and a number of the poets have been jailed for their writing, this anthology reminds us why poetry continues to be a necessary and urgent art form, a challenge to rigid ways of thinking and oppressive governments.

Ming Di is to be commended for gathering together such a powerful selection of poems, which made this reader, at least, thirst for more. What else has Yu Xiuhua, Xu Lizhi, or the gay poet, Mu Cao, written? What other poems did the women in this anthology write?

Ming Di, in chronicling the history of free verse and ongoing new formalism in China, introduces readers to a rich, diverse, exciting, defiant group of poets. She answers many questions even as she raises many more, which is exactly what an anthology of poetry should do. I am very proud to be the publisher of this book.

JOHN YAU
August 2018

Foreword

NEW POETRY WAS A MOVEMENT started in 1917 in Beijing by Hu Shi, a returned student from the US, whose ambition was to change the literary landscape in China. Apparently influenced by the modernist art in New York City and Anglo-American free verse while he was a student at Columbia University, he wrote a long free verse poem in 1916 as an argument during the fierce and lengthy debate he had with his fellow Chinese students regarding free verse vs. classical poetry and this obscure poem became the first free verse in vernacular language (plain speech) in the history of Chinese literature. And we are still writing in his shadow today.

As part of the movement, Hu Shi published "A Preliminary Proposal for Literary Reform" and eight free verse poems in the *New Youth* journal in February 1917 and returned to China in July 1917 to promote the free verse, and soon he became one of the most important intellectuals during the New Cultural Movement in 1919. Since the downfall of the Qing Dynasty in 1912, the Republic of China had gone through many upheavals. The cultural reform was instrumental in driving China into modernity. Also in 1919, Hu Shi published an essay "On New Poetry" and thus named the free verse New Poetry. He proposed that poetry should be written in plain language, not to be bound by the old rigid forms. Plain language was found in ancient poetry as well; Hu Shi's revolution was against the "eight-legged style" of language in seventeenth- to nineteenth-century China. Besides

Hu Shi and the American influence, other overseas Chinese students also brought back to China the Romanticism from the UK and Surrealist poetry from France. Chinese poetry was heading toward freedom in form and individualism in language, leaving behind the classical forms and language along with feudalism.

What was Chinese poetry like before the New Poetry? With three thousand years of literary tradition, the free forms and colloquial speech were regulated in the first anthology compiled by Yin Jifu and edited by Confucius, *The Book of Songs*, a gathering of poems from the eleventh to sixth century BCE where the earliest poems were mostly arranged in four characters a line, with end rhymes, easy to chant and easy to pass on over generations. Qu Yuan (343–278 BCE) from the Chu Kingdom (1042–223 BCE) began writing epic poems in a style that had more variations, four or five words a line, rhymed or unrhymed. Then Chinese poetry developed into more regulated forms, five or seven characters a line with tonal and metrical systems and rhyming schemes, of which Tang Dynasty (about 618–907 CE) produced the best examples. Song Dynasty (960–1279) was the next golden era where a new kind of poetry, *Ci*, with various patterns of syllables and rhymes appeared. After that, drama and prose began to flourish in Ming Dynasty (1368–1644) and Qing Dynasty (1644–1912).

New Poetry as against the classical poetry in the Tang-Song forms has been the avant-garde trend from the 1920s to 1940s; in the 1970s with the Misty Poets emerging; and in the 1980–90s with the Third Generation rising up and continuing through the 21st century— while classical poetry has never died out completely. As we celebrate the one hundredth-year anniversary of New Poetry, there is a revival of classical poetry impelled by the new administration. Many poets have actually been experimenting with the classical language for a decade but for aesthetic reasons such as what Li Sen and Jiang Hao have been practicing, a neoclassical poetry with self-invented forms. The deeper desire is to get rid of the Mao language, which prevailed from 1949 to the present, by revitalizing the elegant language in ancient texts in a renewed style. This renewal of the archaic language and imageries started with Zhang Zao and Cheng Dongdong in the 1980s and Xiao Kaiyu in the 1990s, which differs from the current return to the old forms. Will the forceful return to classical poetry lead to a burst of a new wave of New Poetry?

The anniversary is taking us to a new conjunction. New Poetry will most likely push forward as it has been the avant-garde force for a hundred years. To use Zhuang Zi's saying about "Kun-fish Peng-bird", New Poetry is a giant bird *Peng* transformed from the giant fish *Kun*, the classical poetry. A bird will not go back to the sea but flies on farther and farther. As *Peng* has a long way to go, we will keep challenging the tradition by continuing to "make it new." This anthology is a modest attempt to present some of the achievements of New Poetry in the last one hundred years with a focus on the poets who have been actively engaged in poetry in the recent thirty years. Many of the important poems or poets are translated into English for the first time, such as the first free verse in Chinese by Hu Shi dated 1916; Gen Zi, the first poet of Bei Dao's generation; and poets who have been rediscovered such as Zhu Yingdan, Chen Jingrong, Wu Xinghua, Luo Yihe, Liu Xia, etc., poets who have been underrated such as Chang Yao, Song Wei, Mo Mo, Li Sen, Chen Jun; and many younger poets who are trying to change the way poetry is written in Chinese.

While the mainstream poetry circle in China celebrates the centennial anniversary in 2017, i.e. from 1917 to 2017, using the publication of Hu Shi's eight free verse in 1917 as the beginning, we have traced back to 1916 as the outbreak of New Poetry, as discussed further in the Afterword—"From Butterflies to Living Words: Rereading Hu Shi." Since many of the literary movements in China have been outlined in more details in *New Cathay: Contemporary Chinese Poetry* (Tupelo Press, 2013), we focus on two traditions in this anthology: the Poetry of Plain Speech from Hu Shi's vernacular language to the Spoken Language Poetry by Yu Jian and Yi Sha; and the Reformed

Formalism from Wen Yiduo to Yang Lian and Jiang Hao. It might be an ambitious approach to present both the Revolution of free verse and the ongoing Renaissance in China as they often intertwined and battled with each other. The new formalists resist the "vernacular" language in an attempt to re-create a new language that sounds ancient and contemporary at the same time as exemplified by the work of Zhang Zao as mentioned earlier and that of Yang Lian, Song Wei, Jiang Hao, and Chen Jun.

There are fifty-six nationalities in China but most anthologies of modern Chinese poetry contain works primarily by the Han writers. We have tried to change that by promoting "minority" poets. Of the 120 authors from all corners of China gathered in this anthology, there are some, although far from enough, ethnic "minority" poets that I would like to highlight here:

Yi: Jidi Majia and Jike Bu

Manchu: Wang Xiaoni and Na Ye

Tibetan: Kawa Niangji and Xi Wa

Muslim (Hui ethnicity): Ma Yan

Mongolian: Su Xiaoyan

However, most of these poets write in Chinese. Due to the "unification" policy in terms of languages and writings carried out in China since the first emperor, Qin (pronounced Chin), and throughout Chinese history, many of the minority languages are dying out even though there have been efforts to recover the languages. Another issue is that it's difficult to find avant-garde poetry in the ethnic communities in China. There seems to be a conflict of aesthetics between modernism and traditional folk poetry as most of the experimental poets happen to be Han. There is also difficulty in finding language experts who are also poets. We are hoping that with the growing number of bilingual poets in China, i.e. poets who write in Chinese and their own ethnic language, more poetry from the ethnic communities will be translated in the future so that Western readers will see a more diversified China through poetry.

"Omissions are not accidents." Several earlier celebrities such as Lu Xun, Guo Moruo, Xu Zhimo, and Ai Qing are left out to give more space to those more relevant today such as Wen Yiduo, Fei Ming, Bian Zhilin and Mu Dan and to include more poets from the recent thirty years. Geographically, important poets from Taiwan, Hong Kong, and overseas are also included, presenting a broader view of how New Poetry or Modern Chinese Poetry started and evolved. A few poets might be considered controversial for political reasons, such as Huang Xiang, Liu Xiaobo, and Liao Yiwu who are included along with poets holding government positions such as Jidi Majia and Chen Xianfa and many government-sponsored poets such as Lei Pingyang, Shen Wei, and Li Yuansheng. This is to present some of the political diversities. It is interesting to compare Liu Xiaobo and Mo Yan, both born in 1955, both educated at Beijing Normal University (BNU), one was awarded the Nobel Peace Prize in 2010 and the other the Nobel Prize in Literature in 2012, and both write poetry besides prose and literary criticism (Liu Xiaobo) and fiction (Mo Yan). There's also a balance of the "spoken language poets" and "intellectual poets." It's not a superficial attempt to have a broad range of voices, but an effort to look at varied aesthetics as well as any underlying ideological differences. All the poems are carefully selected to show the richness and complexities of New Poetry over the last one hundred years within the limited pages of this anthology.

Language and form have been two of the major concerns for experimental poets in the last one hundred years. Poets from the New Moon group in the 1920s to 1940s explored a reformed classical way of writing modern poetry. They experimented with new meters and new rhyming patterns as demonstrated in this anthology. 1949 to 1976 is called "twenty-seven years" of political poetry. In the late 1970s through the early '80s, the Misty Poets rose against the mainstream poetry but were using the same language, which they fought against and in the same high lofty tone. The Third Generation that emerged in the mid-1980s began to challenge both the Misty poetry and the mainstream poetry. They went back beyond the Tang-Song forms and went deeper into the earlier Chinese poetry: they found a new poetic language by blending the ancient texts with present day conversational speech. It is by looking at this very transformation that I realize *Peng* is not just a bird. but a bird reborn from the fish *Kun*. It flies up high but carries features of *Kun* even though it will never be *Kun* again.

MING DI
October 2017, August 2018
Beijing and Los Angeles

Major Events in the Last One Hundred Years

1911 Qing Dynasty overthrown by the 1911 Revolution

1912 Republic of China (ROC) established

1915 Chinese students in the US debating on literary reform; Ezra Pound published *Cathay*, translations of classical Chinese poetry

1916 Hu Shi wrote the first free-verse poem in vernacular Chinese and published "To Chen Duxiu—Eight Don'ts for Literary Revolution" in *New Youth* journal edited by Chen Duxiu

1917 Hu Shi published "A Preliminary Proposal for Literary Reform" and eight free-verse poems in *New Youth*; Hu Shi returned to China in July to promote New Poetry; T. S. Eliot published the essay "Reflections on Vers Libre"

1918 Hu Shi joined *New Youth*

1919 May Fourth New Cultural Movement burst out; *New Youth* editing members splitting into radical leftists (pro-communism) and conservative rightists; Hu Shi protesting the journal as propaganda for Soviet Russia and communism; Hu Shi published an essay titled "On New Poetry"

1920 Hu Shi published his first book of New Poetry, *Experiments*

1921 China's Communist Party (CCP) established by Chen Duxiu who was purged by the party in 1927

1922 Wen Yiduo went to Chicago to study art, and returned to China in 1925 to promote formalism and neoclassical poetry

1923 New Moon Society founded (free verse, then formalist)

1924 Rabindranath Tagore visited China

1932 *Modernism* journal founded, Chinese modernist circle formed

1938 W. H. Auden visited China during WWII

1949 China Writers Association founded under the leadership of China's Communist Party; People's Republic of China (PRC) established, ROC moved to Taiwan

1957 Mao Zedong launched the Anti-Rightist Movement

1966 Mao Zedong launched the Cultural Revolution

1969 Mang Ke, Duo Duo and Gen Zi went to Baiyangdian farm outside Beijing; Baiyangdian Poetry circle formed in 1972

1976 Mao Zedong died; Cultural Revolution ended

1978 Beijing Democratic Wall, first democratic movement after 1949; Huang Xiang launched *Enlighten* journal in Guizhou; Mang Ke and Bei Dao launched *Jintian* journal in Beijing and Misty Poetry circle formed (name was given later)

1981 *Anthology of Nine Leaves* published (poems by nine poets who were active in the 1940s such as Mu Dan, Chen Jingrong, Zheng Min, etc. who also founded *New Poetry Journal* in the 1940s)

1986 Exhibition of contemporary Modernist schools and circles; Third Generation emerged (here Third Generation is a general term referring to the Post-Misty Poets, while "first generation" refer to Hu Shi and all the poets of New Poetry before 1949)

1989 Tiananmen Students Movement for Democracy

1997 Hong Kong returned to China from the UK

1999 Debate between folk poetry and intellectual writing

2013 *Canon of One Hundred Year Chinese New Poetry* published by Yangtze River Publishing House of Arts and Literature (thirty volumes, 300 poets included)

2014 Xi Jinping delivered Beijing Talk on Literature and Art modeled after Mao Zedong's Yan'an Talk on Literature and Art in 1942; Xi Jinping promoting "Chinese Values"

2015 Mainstream establishment started to promote classical poetry, *Poetry* journal launched Chen Zi'ang Poetry Prize awarding 100000 RMB to the best poet of the year and 300000 RMB to the best classical poem of the year

2017 Many poets and scholars in China celebrate 100 years of New Poetry acknowledging Hu Shi as the first writer of New Poetry but still ignoring his groundbreaking poem from 1916 that we introduced in this anthology

New Poetry from China

1917–2017

Hu Shi 胡适

Hu Shi or **Hu Shih (1891–1962)**, born in 1891 in Anhui province, started writing classical poetry at a very young age. He went to Cornell University in 1910 as an undergraduate and then to Columbia University for PhD in philosophy. He returned to China to teach at Beijing University in 1917 and promote New Poetry. He was ambassador to the US from 1938 to 1942, and chancellor of Beijing University from 1946 to 1948. He moved to Taiwan in 1949 and died there in 1962. February 1917 is generally regarded as the starting point of New Poetry when Hu Shi published eight free verse poems. However, his long debate-in-verse from his diary dated July 22, 1916, translated here, is much more interesting and should be considered as the first attempt of New Poetry.

REPLY TO OLD MEI—A POEM IN PLAIN SPEECH

Days are getting cool, people less busy,
Old Mei starts a fight and accuses Hu Shi
of being too ridiculous in saying
that "Living literature is what China needs,"
that "Writing must be in the way people talk!"
Who says there are living words and dead words?
Isn't the vernacular too vulgar?

. . .

Old Mei complains, while Hu Shi laughs out loud.
Cool down man, how can you talk so loud
with such an outdated tone?

Words may not be old or new, but definitely dead
or alive.
Ancient people say Yu, we say Yao (to desire).
Ancient people say Zhi, we say Dao (to arrive).
Ancient people say Ni, we say Niao (to pee).
Same words, a little change in the sound.
Why call it vulgar?
Why even argue?
Ancient people say letters, we say characters.
Ancient people hang on poles, we hang on beams.

   ...

Not only words, but also texts.
Dead or alive.
A living text is what you know and can talk about.
A dead text is what you have to translate.
Texts of three thousand years, up and down, living or dead,
who knows how many have been hijacked.
Look at the Shangshu.
It becomes fiction.
Look at Songs of Qingyun.
It becomes drama.

   ...

Look at the texts of Han Tang,
same as the Latin you're learning.

   ...

How can there be anyone so stupid
as not to be in love with living beauties
but instead hug those ice-cold skeletons.
Old Mei jumps up: This is absurd!
If what you say is true,
all peasants are poets.

   ...

Days are getting hot, people busier.
Old Mei doodles with ink, gets angrier.
But revolution of texts involves both of us.
I dare not argue, nor dare ignore.
I have to speak out. Not speaking out is not a way out.
Don't you dare laugh
at a poem in plain speech. It beats
a hundred books of the Southern Society texts.

June 22, 1916
(Excerpt from a longer poem)
MD, KSK

Southern Society mentioned toward the end of this poem was a big literary society in the early twentieth-century China, established in 1909 and dissolved in 1923. The society helped the 1911 Revolution in overthrowing the Qing Dynasty but most of its members wrote in classical language, i.e. politically open-minded but literarily conservative. Hu Shi was criticizing the latter.

Wen Yiduo 闻一多

WEN YIDUO (1899–1946) was an important poet and critic in the early stage of New Poetry. He was born in Hubei but educated in Beijing. He went to Chicago in 1922 to study art but became a poet. He returned to China in 1925 to promote the musical structure and visual beauty of poetry. He became one of the first neoclassical poets and a primary force in promoting a reformed formal poetry in China. He was dean of the college of liberal arts at Wuhan University. He published two collections of poetry (in 1922 and 1928) and several groundbreaking research projects on the *Book of Changes*, *Book of Songs*, *Zhuang Zi*, *Book of Chu Ci* (including Qu Yuan's poetry) and *Du Fu* which shed light on our understanding of the classical masterpieces. At the request of Robert Payne, he compiled the first anthology of Chinese modern poetry to be translated into English but before it was published, he was assassinated by the Kuomintang government during the Chinese civil war.

PERHAPS—AN ELEGY

Far too long you've been weeping.
Perhaps you should've been sleeping.
Don't let the night hawk cough,
or bats fly about, or frogs buzz off.

Don't let sunlight open your eyes as you know how.
Don't let a cool breeze brush your eyebrows.
No one will wake you up, which is perfectly fine.
To shelter your sleep I'll hold the umbrella of a pine.

Perhaps you hear worms digging through
the dirt, or roots of small grass slurping the dew.
Perhaps you are listening to music more captivating
than the harsh jangle of human cursing.

Close your eyelids and close them deep.
I will let you sleep. I will let you sleep.
I'll cover you lightly with yellow earth
and let paper money burn for a new birth.

1928
MD

Li Jinfa　李金发

Known as "Baudelaire in China," **LI JINFA (1900–1976)** was born in Guangdong, went to France in 1919 to study art and returned to China in 1925. He sent two collections of poems to friends in China in 1923, which were highly praised and influential, resulting in the birth of modernism in China. He worked as a diplomat in Iran and Iraq in the 1940s and spent his later years in the US.

LAMENT

Like fallen leaves splattering
blood on our
feet,
life is a smile
on the lips
of death.

Under the half-dead moon
you drink and sing
with a cracking throat,
your voice howling in the north wind—
hush!
—to comfort the one you love who's leaving.

Open the doors and windows,
be shameful,
let dust cover the eyes
of love.

Are you shy,
or angry at life?

Like fallen leaves splattering
blood on our feet, life is but a smile
on the lips of death.

1923
MD, KSK

Fei Ming   废名

FEI MING (1901–1967) was born Feng Wenbing in Hubei. He started publishing poems and essays in 1922 while attending Beijing University. He was a major writer in Beijing and was influential for his prose style and for being "a true Chinese New Poet without Western influence." During the Sino-Japanese war when most poets in Beijing moved to Southwestern Associated University in Kunming, he returned to his hometown in Hubei to teach and was called back to Beijing when the war was over. He was also an accomplished scholar of New Poetry with a valuable collection of *Lectures on New Poetry*. He was rediscovered in the 1990s, and since then has been acclaimed for his Zen poems.

THE NIGHT OF DECEMBER 19TH

Deep night is a lamp on trees,
a stream running down a high mountain,
an ocean outside your body.
The starry sky is a forest of birds,
flowers, fish.
It's a heavenly dream.
The ocean—a mirror of things tonight.
Thinking is beauty,
a home,
the sun, the moon,
the day and month,
a light,

a fire—
the shadow on the wall,
the sound of a winter night.

1936
MD

Feng Zhi 冯至

FENG ZHI (1905–1993) published his first poem in 1924 while a college student in Beijing. He then went to Germany to study art, literature and philosophy, and returned to China in 1936. His well-known *27 Sonnets* came out in 1941 during the wartime in China. After that he became widely known for the reformed Fourteen Liners that he invented, still popular in China, i.e. fourteen lines of free verse with free rhymes. He was honored with many awards in his later years for his translation of German poetry.

CRY FROM THE WILDERNESS

I often see a village boy
or a peasant woman in the wilderness
cry up into the sky, speechless.
Is it for a punishment, or

a damaged toy?
For her son's illness
or her dead husband, helpless?
They cry, non-stop, or

as if their whole life were caught
in the cry, no other life
or anything else outside.

They cry and cry, not aware
of how long, their tears flowing in the air
for a world of despair.

1941
MD

Dai Wangshu　戴望舒

DAI WANGSHU (1905–1950) was a poet and translator from Zhejiang. He went to study in France in 1932 and returned to China in 1935, becoming a prominent poet in the 1940's and a well-known translator of French poetry. In 1936, he founded *New Poetry* monthly with his friends, which only lasted a year with 10 issues published but was very influential as a joint platform for the new formal poetry from the New Moon circle and modern poetry from the Chinese modernists.

AT THE TOMB OF XIAO HONG

I've walked six lonely hours
to bring you a red camellia.
I'm waiting. The night is long. But
you turn to the waves, casual and familiar.

(1944)
MD

Xiao Hong (1911–1942), as mentioned in the title of this poem, was an important woman writer, known for her novels about northern China. She died of illness in Hong Kong during the Sino-Japanese war. This poem by Dai Wangshu in memory of her has been regarded by contemporary poets in China as the best short poem before 1949. It's not sentimental as most of Dai's poems tend to be. It's rhymed but without the tonal metrical scheme as in classical poetry. The pause in the third line brings freshness to the ear.

Bian Zhilin 卞之琳

A poet that bridged the modern to contemporary, Western influence to Chinese tradition, **BIAN ZHILIN (1910–2000)** started writing poetry while in college in the 1930s. He was a research fellow at Oxford University from 1947–1949, taught at Beijing University 1949–1952, and later worked at the Academy of Social Science, becoming vice-chairman of the Shakespeare Society in China. He won the "Lifetime Achievement in Poetry" in 2000. This short poem is a fragment from a long poem by Bian Zhilin who only saved this fragment as Ezra Pound did with "In a Station of the Metro." It has become a modern classic, the most quoted of all his poems. It's the change of perception and subtlety that's been critiqued over the years.

FRAGMENT

You stand on the bridge to watch the view
when someone upstairs watches you.

The moon swaddles you with a clear beam
while you adorn the other's dream.

1935
MD

Ji Xian 纪弦

Ji Xian (1913–2013), the last modernist poet from the 1930s whose death on July 22, 2013 seemed to have marked the ending of the vernacular free verse started by Hu Shi on July 22, 1916. The longing for a new form of poetry as expressed by the New Moon poets in the 1920s has become stronger. But since many poets of the Third Generation (Post-Misty Poets) have become the primary writers in China, New Poetry has been promoted again and pushed further in recent years. Ji Xian was born in Hebei province as Lu Yu, and grew up in Jiangsu. He started writing poetry at age sixteen and then changed style after meeting Dai Wangshu (also in this anthology) who made him a poet of modern free verse. He was actively involved in poetry activities and launching magazines in the 1930s. He moved around frequently, from Anhui to Hong Kong, to Shanghai, to Taiwan, and finally to San Francisco in 1976 where he lived till he died at age one hundred. As one of the early modernist poets in Taiwan in the 1950s, his influence spread to mainland China in the early 21st century.

CITY OF FIRE

From this window I see your soul,
a deep, dark, dangerous sea. I see a city of fire,
no firearms, water hose, or water—
just waves of madmen and women, naked.

I hear my name in the surging chaos,
ripples of echoes, unending, my name

my love's name enemy's name living names
dead names dead living love's names.

When I whisper I'm here, a nerve reaction
unruly, I become a city of fire instantly.

MD

Zhu Yingdan   朱英诞

ZHU YINGDAN (1913–1983) was an active poet in the 1940s, a member of the Fei Ming circle in Beijing, but was out of the limelight for decades (as he didn't publish a single poem after 1949) until he was rediscovered in recent years. He wrote several thousand poems, a sequel of *Lectures on New Poetry* (after Fei Ming, compiled by Chen Jun in 2008) and an autobiography that documented the history of New Poetry. Chen Jun wrote his PhD dissertation on Zhu Yingdan and promoted his poetry which has found many serious readers. A collection of his poems will be published soon, compiled by Chen Jun who is also in this anthology.

I'M AFRAID TO THINK

Watermarks in the galaxy—so gentle.
But the gentlest wind— the night travelers.
Look, those city lights,
the buildings made of stars,
silent. I'm afraid to think
that there are gardens
falling out of sight.
In your smallest dreams I fall,
quiet.

Stars drift, one by one,
all solitary, treasures of the night,
in proper distance of each other

like acquaintances, or cold tombstones.
Moonlight is dust and if so, mystifies
your beautiful eyes.

(1943)
MD

Chen Jingrong　陈敬蓉

CHEN JINGRONG (1917–1989) was born into a wealthy family in Sichuan, went to high school, and ran away from home at age fifteen. She moved around the country and was self-taught in English, French and Russian, and worked as translator and literary editor. In 1946 she met a group of poets in Shanghai which later became the legendary *Nine Leaves* group. She published two books of poetry in 1948. After 1949 she became a translator for the *World Literature* journal in Beijing. Her translation of Baudelaire influenced two generations of Chinese poets such as Duo Duo and Bai Hua.

SPRING FOR THE LOGICAL PATIENT

There are streams that run
as if not running.
There are wheels that turn
as if not turning at all.
There are faces that smile too much
as if crying.
When the light is too strong,
you will not see it
as if invisible, as if it were darkness.
Completely perfect means defective.
Being full is equal to emptiness.
The maximum is the smallest,
zero is infinity.
The world is ancient but fresh,

forever fresh and new;
taking out your grandmother's wardrobe
you can open a chic boutique.

1947
MD, KSK

Mu Dan　穆旦

MU DAN (1918–1977), pen name for Zha Liangzheng, was an important poet and translator in China. He was originally from Tianjin and started publishing at age sixteen. He went to the University of Chicago in 1949 and returned to China in 1953. He was persecuted in 1958 and during the Cultural Revolution (1966–1976), but continued writing poetry until he died of heart attack.

FLY

A fly, a small one,
flits in the sunlight here and there.
How do you find three meals a day?
How do you?
Where do you hide to escape
storms?
The world is always new
and you are always curious.
Alive, you happily fly,
half-starved, but lively,
sniffing here and there, looking around
ignoring what people may think.
You find sweet honey
where we hold our noses.
You see yourself equal to humans,
and you sing to the summer—
attracted by an illusion,

an ideal.
You fly in the door, and out the window,
enduring your own wild flapping.

1975
MD, KSK

Zheng Min   郑敏

ZHENG MIN (1920–) was born in Fujian, graduated from Southwest United University in 1943, and then went to study literature and philosophy at Brown University in the US, earning a master's degree in 1952. She returned to China in 1955 and taught at Beijing Normal University from 1960 until her retirement in 2006. Influenced by Feng Zhi and Rilke as translated by Feng Zhi, Zheng Min started writing poetry while a student in college and published her work in the 1940s during the war time in China. She is the last living member of the *Nine Leaves* group of poets from the 1940s whose work was published in 1981 as a collection of nine poets, titled *Book of Nine Leaves*.

GOLDEN RICE SHEAVES

Golden rice stands in sheaves
in the newly cut autumn field.
I think of droves of exhausted mothers,
I see rugged faces along the road at dusk.
On the day of harvest, a full moon hangs
atop the towering trees,
and in the twilight, distant mountains
approach my heart.
Nothing is more quiet than this, a statue,
shouldering so much weariness—
you lower your head in thought
in the unending autumn field.
Silence. Silence. History is nothing

but a small stream flowing under your feet.
You stand where the rice is, your thought
becoming a thought of the human race.

1943
MD, KSK

Wu Xinghua   吴兴华

WU XINGHUA (1921–1966) was a highly gifted poet, scholar and translator. He published a long poem at age sixteen by exploring a third way, not the realism as promoted by the left wing, nor modernism by the avant-garde poets, but a reformed formal poetry or modernized classical poetry. He went to Yanjing University and became a faculty member there after graduation. He was the first to translate Joyce's *Ulysses* into Chinese. He was also known for his translation of Dante's *Divine Comedy* and Shakespeare's play, *Henry IV*. He was persecuted by Red Guards during the Cultural Revolution and died at age forty-five.

UNTITLED

Do not let me see the beautiful tears
over ruins for a memory I can't bear.
Ravens fly, the mournful sound of flutes
lingers for decades. Heroic fireflies flutter
toward lights looking for things lost on their way.
Yesterday's sunset half hidden in haze?
Oh this sadness, this fear. Why are you staying?
The unpredicted arrival, her barely accepted saying.
Will one word on her lips be the source next year
of endlessly flowing regretfully shameful tears?

1940s
MD

Lü Yuan 绿原

Lü Yuan (1922–2009) was born in Hubei, exiled to Chongqing during the World War II, and spent later years in Beijing as a prominent translator and editor. As a poet, he won the Golden Wreath Award of the Struga International Poetry Festival in 1998.

FIREFLY

The moth dies by the candle
that's dying out in the wind—

a green light
glowing in the fog, a cold light,
undying in the rainy night.
How should I really sing for you—

you're your own lighthouse
for your own path.

MD

Luo Fu 洛夫

Luo Fu (1928–2018) was born in Hunan as Mo Luofu, went to Taiwan in 1949, and became one of the early modernist poets there. Together with Zhang Mo and Ya Xian, he founded the Genesis Poetry Society in 1954 in Taiwan and was an editor for forty years. In 1996 he moved to Canada and lived there as an immigrant writer. His poetry has been influential in Taiwan, mainland China and diaspora communities.

CRAB CLAW FLOWERS

Perhaps you have no sorrows
when the crab claws crawl along the clay pot.
They explode when they bloom
and they look back in silence.
At the window in the deep red of despair
you gesture toward me.
You speak from the tangling blue knots: bare buds
bloom—fragrance spills from their
bodies. One petal, another.
Crab claw flowers
hanging horizontally
occupy the whole sky on your forehead.

In a most wondrous moment you say: pain.
Leaves open, roots in the water.
You are startled:
you recognize yourself
as the flowers open like a wound.

1985
MD, KSK

Guan Guan 管管

GUAN GUAN's real name is Guan Yunlong, one of the very few poets of his generation still alive. He was born in Qingdao in 1929, and went to Taiwan with the nationalist army in 1941. After he retired from military service, he joined the modernist circle of poets in Taiwan. He is still productive in writing as of today.

WASHING HAIR IN MOONLIGHT

She dares to put her head outside of the window
letting the moonlight wash her hair.
But a head like that is to be plucked!
She washes and washes, her head following the moon.
Might as well let the moon dash down quickly to be her head.
Why not!
But a headless body can scare people to death!
But a body shouldering a moon
walking around
can also scare people to death. Look at that guy flat on the
    ground—
he's been scared to death.

MD, KSK

Shang Qin 商禽

SHANG QIN (1930–2010), born in Sichuan, mainland China, lived in Taiwan since 1950. He was one of the early modernist poets in Taiwan, nominated for the Nobel Prize once. He was a pioneer of prose poems and was widely known for surrealism in his writing.

GIRAFFE

The young prison guard notices at the monthly physical
checkups that all the prisoners have grown taller
from the back of their necks. He reports to the warden:
"Sir, the windows are too high!"
But the answer is: "No, they're looking up at Time."

The kindhearted young guard doesn't know what Time
    looks like,
nor its origin or whereabouts. So night after night
he patrols the zoo, guarding the giraffe bars.

MD, KSK

Zheng Chouyu 郑愁予

ZHENG ZHAOYUAN was born in Shandong in 1933. He went to Taiwan in 1949, and moved to the US in 1968 to attend the International Writing Program at the University of Iowa. He taught Chinese at Yale University until he retired to Taiwan in 2005. He published his first book of poetry at age sixteen, followed by eight more. He has won the New Poetry Prize and the Time's Literary Award in Taiwan.

MISTAKEN

While passing through the Southland,
I see you, a lovely face, awaiting, blossom and fade
away like a lotus. The East wind hasn't blown
this way, willows wave without March's catkins.
Your heart has become a castle, withdrawn,
a street of mossy stones facing sunsets
with no sound of footsteps. Spring's curtain is drawn,
your heart is a window that opens only to you alone.
Clip clop! I stop by your castle on a horse, mistaken for
    another—
for a beautiful reason. Alas, I'm not
the home-returning guy, but only
a traveler passing by.

1954
MD, KSK

Chang Yao 昌耀

CHANG YAO (1936–2000) was born in Hunan and moved to Qinghai Province in 1955, from where he was exiled to the countryside in 1958 during the Anti-Rightist Movement in China and then was reinstated in 1979. He began publishing poetry in 1954 and committed suicide in 2000. He is newly rediscovered and widely praised today.

EAGLE, SNOW, SHEPHERD

An eagle summons a leaden wind
and soars from the peak of an ice mountain.
Frosty air shakes free
from its drumming wings.

In the mist, hoarier and thicker,
the eagle disappears.
Shepherds on the grassland bare their arms,
and lifting up their swords,
taste the first snow.

1956
MD, KSK

Huang Xiang   黄翔

HUANG XIANG (1941–) is one of the earliest avant-garde poets in contemporary China, even earlier than the X Poetry Society (Guo Shiying, etc.) in the 1960s and the Misty Poets such as Bei Dao in the 1970s. He was born in Hunan, and moved to Guizhou in 1956 to become a factory worker. He started publishing poetry in 1958, and his poem "Solo" written in 1962 was distinctively different from the mainstream poetry. He founded an independent poetry journal, *Enlighten,* and went to Beijing to promote it in 1978 and there he became one of the pioneer poets for the Beijing Democratic Wall (1978-1979). He was jailed numerous times from 1959 to 1990. He moved to America in 1997, and in 2004 he became the first poet in residence in the City of Asylum in Pittsburgh.

ENCOUNTER

from a tree
fall small pieces
of a shattered
sun
a leopard spreads a land of waste
on its spotted face

1982
MD

Luo Qing 罗青

Luo Qing was born in Qingdao in 1948 and brought to Taiwan by his parents in 1949. He started to paint at age sixteen and started writing poetry in college. He then went to Washington State University to study comparative literature and later returned to teach in Taiwan. He is the first postmodernist poet in Chinese. He lives between Shanghai and Taiwan.

MOTIVATION

A persimmon
stands up
suddenly in my messy breakfast tray

and salutes me
like a beyond-this-cold-mountain sunrise
that surprises me. It turns
into a storm of mist and gradually

disperses around me
erasing its own last
single
trace
slowly slo lo o . . .

From the sequence of
"An Interdisciplinary Study of Persimmons"
MD

Bei Dao 北岛

BEI DAO (nom de plume of Zhao Zhenkai), born in 1948 in Beijing, was the best known of the Misty Poets in China. (He doesn't like the term "Misty" but prefers to use "Today Circle" for the poets that emerged in the 1970s.) With Mang Ke, he founded the independent journal *Jintian* (*Today*) in 1978, one of the fifty independent journals that emerged in China from 1978 to 1981. He went into exile in 1989, returned to Hong Kong in 2007, and founded Hong Kong International Poetry Nights in 2009. He won the Golden Wreath Award of the Struga Poetry Evenings in 2015.

JUNE

Wind says into my ear: June
June, a blacklist I missed
in time

Be aware of the way we say goodbye
the sigh within the words

Be aware of the annotations:
The plastic flowers
over the left bank of death
The square of cement extends
from writing to

now, this very moment
I run

from writing
as dawn's hammered out
a flag covering the sea

and a loudspeaker loyal to the deep bass
of sea says: June

MD

Liang Bingjun 梁秉钧

Born in Guangdong but grew up in Hong Kong, **LIANG BINGJUN (1949-2013)**, aka Ping-kwan Leung (who also writes under his pen name Yesi), was an important writer in Hong Kong and in Chinese language literature with many volumes of poetry, fiction, and essays published. He was also one of the first to introduce French literature and Latin American literature to Hong Kong and Taiwan readers in the early 1970s. He earned a PhD in comparative literature from the University of California in San Diego in 1984. He was the recipient of the Thumb's Poetry Award in 1983 and 1991. He also won the inaugural Hong Kong Biennial Awards for Chinese Literature in 1990. He was a DAAD fellow in Berlin in 1998.

TEA

No faces rise
from this cup of tea,
only tea leaf stems swirl
saying friends will visit.
I count little lights in the warm brown tea—
eyes in tranquility
like stars in the summer night
approaching from the front gate of the sky
and disappearing to the back door of clouds.
In between, all that floats parts as well.

Not a moment to calm down
or drink tea face to face.

We sigh and find our occasional meetings
like the fragrance of tea in the distance.
A hand lifts the cup,
a shadow sways inside.
There's always a bitterness in tea
that jasmine petals gather and disperse
in certain shapes.

1973
MD, KSK

Mang Ke 芒克

MANG KE (pen name for Jiang Shiwei) was born in Shengyang in 1953 but grew up in Beijing. He was one of the early avant-garde poets in contemporary China along with Duo Duo and Gen Zi. In 1978 he and Bei Dao founded an independent journal *Jintian* (Today). Currently he lives in Beijing as an artist.

SUNFLOWER IN THE SUN

Do you see it?
Do you see the sunflower in the sun?
Look, it doesn't bow
but turns its head back
as if to bite
the rope around its neck
held by the sun.
Do you see it?
Do you see the sunflower, head up,
gazing at the sun?
Its head almost eclipses the sun.
But even when there is no sun
it glows.
Do you see the sunflower?
You should get closer.
Getting close you'll find
the soil beneath its feet.
Each handful of soil
oozes with blood.

1988
MD, KSK

Duo Duo 多多

Duo Duo (pen name of Li Shizheng), born in Beijing in 1951, is the most prominent poet in contemporary China, one of the Misty Poets along with Bei Dao and Mang Ke, and the first poet to experiment with a new language when he wrote "People rise from cheese" in 1973. He lived in exile for fifteen years from 1989 until returning to China in 2004, winning the prestigious Chinese Literature Awards from the Southern Media Group in the same year. He started teaching at Hainan University in 2004 and retired in 2016. In 2010, he was awarded the Neustadt International Prize for Literature from the US. Currently he lives in Beijing.

PROMISE

I love—I love my shadow,
a parrot, I love to eat what it loves
to eat. I love to give you what I don't have.
I love to ask you do you still love me?
I love your ears that love to hear that I love

adventures. I love the house on fire, inviting us
to lie down as its roof.
I love to lie on my side, casting a straight evening shade,
a line of small villages for a full body.
I love your lips to be close and to know my promise.

I love my dreams full of intelligent ambitions
like a real groom.

I love to eat raw meat, looking straight into hell.
But I love more to play violin in your arms.
I love to turn off the lights early, and wait for your body
to light the room.

I love to sleep while my pillow grows plums.
When I wake up, they grow back on their tree branches.
I love the waves that love the front deck all night long.
I love to cry out "Come back" and you will.
I love to torture the harbor and torture the words.

I love to control myself at a desk.
I love to put my hands into the sea.
I love my fingers all stretched out
holding fast to the edge of a wheat field.
I love my five fingers being your five boyfriends

as before. I love memory to be a bit of life, not much,
but more than it can lose when a woman walks up to me,
as she did thirty years ago—
in the sunset, a girl with a violin case
smiled at me for no reason.

I love even more when we're still a pair of torpedoes
waiting to shoot again.
I love to join you in the deep ocean, you
are mine and mine alone, and I
still love to say and to sing *I promise*—

2001

MD

THINK OF THIS WORD

This thinking, full empty,
this meaning, the mine, the spellbound,
the force from the coal seam,
the blood seamed deep in the formation,
the intersection where humans are spilled out,
the shake of the left hand, the hole that's left there—
think of this death, this don't-know-how-to-die.

Inside the sand, upright spines are buried,
and on their shoulders are cemeteries and construction
    sites.
Inside the tent, death is too much exposed.
Burial releases a force.
Before that, invested in the pit is the debt to time.
From its center, the pre-death events silently
seep out.
Above the constructed and to-be-constructed wilderness
is the history in which no one
lives in a safety zone.
No watching, no motivation
to watch. But in watching it
we return to it, partially.

This—these variegated promises in the weeds . . .

2007
MD

I'M DREAMING

I'm dreaming of my father as a cloud drawing clouds
left-handed, as if in the glass window of a drugstore.
He wears a blue raincoat, crossing a street
along the spinning needle of an old gramophone.
He passes through a laundromat and a coffin shop
not far from where I grew up.
He walks, and with his blue skeleton
he calls for a streetcar.

I'm dreaming that on every corner stands a father
fighting with fathers. I'm dreaming of him and see
his back among the fathers.
Every street resists his fighting, every corner
is the witness: in the center of the street
a tongue is pulled out like a bicycle tire . . .

Time stops after my father's death, then rushes out
in full swing to the street.
Can someone stop me and wake me up?
No one.
I dream on, as if in a dream of all the dead
dreaming of their entire lives.

Black soil is shoveled into the open chests
of the dead, shovel after shovel, and from their bodies
the land takes its new frontiers.
Flies fly away. They don't eat human flesh any more.
The dead sit up and cry when they see the hooks
in the fish market . . .

I take this as my dream.
I've dreamed what I should've dreamed
and I've dreamed what the dream tells me to dream of
as if my dream is hijacked—

2001

MD

Gen Zi　根子

GEN ZI (pen name for Yue Zhong) was born in Beijing in 1951, a class-mate of Mang Ke and Duo Duo but he started writing poetry before them (although they became more famous than him.) Gen Zi wrote his first poem, *March and Doomsday*, in 1971, followed by eight long poems, and soon stopped writing to become an opera singer because his poetry was censored. Many critics today find his poetry more mature than that of the Misty Poets who emerged around the same time or after him in the 1970s.

MARCH AND DOOMSDAY

March marches into doomsday.
This is the moment that
Spring, the flirtatious hereditary bride of the earth,
wrapped with hot pink dust,
comes for the Nth time, sly and dodging,
making no sound. I've seen nineteen
identical springs
with the same bloody smirk that
arrives in March. This time,
for the twentieth time it takes the earth, my only comrade,
away from underneath my feet, wishing
I would appreciate failure and envy for the twentieth time.
It comes with the warning: "Hey Backbone,
fly up like a cloud."
I'm human with no wings, but I've made
spring lose the race for the first time.

This wedding banquet on earth, this annual disaster—
will certainly resemble its past as in the last nineteen years.
With the menstruation of the prostitute-like spring
it will come again after February. It
will come in March.

She has come indeed,
dodging, with no sound.
My heart is an aging rock, fumigated by nineteen
fierce summers without melting,
cracking, or shifting.
The young grass on the rocks
and the fine gravel have been washed
by the nineteenth blistering rain, burned to death.
Bare rocks, dark, stark, missing
the yellow gloss. Today
my dark brown heart is silent, heavy,
no longer radiant, like a piece of steel, heated and cooled
nineteen times.

. . .

As a friend of the earth, I've been faithful,
trying to stop him nineteen times. He gets excited, saying
"Spring, warm spring, March—what does it mean?"
I've been faithful.
"Spring? This venomous slut. Under her gorgeously pleated
   garment
when didn't she conceal the summer,
this cruel paramour, this devil that carries fire?"
I've been faithful.
"Spring, this ruthless trafficker, after snuggling you and
   fuddling you,

when didn't she release those green robbers
to set fire and burn you to ashes?"
I've been faithful.
"Spring, this frivolous traitor, after you've been burned
and roasted by the summer,
when did she ever rescue you
with tender sincerity? When did she ever
come back to you in July?"
I suffer from humiliation and sacrifice, but
as ignorant as I am, I'm serious, extremely serious.
The anchor chain is mangled and rusted,
while my heart has matured.
It seems that for the first time March has come, wide
    awake.
Sooner or later spring will multiply. Nineteen times two
or even three if there is a chance. It will never
burn my heart to maturity—
a stone apple.

It's March today, the twentieth spring whistles
presumptuously, here and there.
My feet have felt the earth again
stubbornly creeping, its eyes the rivers and lakes
once again blurred, shedding tears of gratitude
or running away like fugitives.

1971
(Excerpt from a long poem)
MD, KSK

Yi Lei 伊蕾

Yɪ Leɪ (1951–2018) was born in Tianjin as Sun Gui-zhen, one of the earliest feminist poets in China. She studied creative writing at the Lu Xun Literary Institute, and Chinese Literature at Beijing University. She published eight collections of poems, among them *A Single Woman's Bedroom*, *The Love Poems of Yi Lei*, and *Women's Age*. A recipient of the Zhuang Zhong Wen Literature Prize, Yi Lei's work has been translated into English, Russian, and other languages. One of Yi Lei's dreams was to travel to a hundred countries. She made it to sixty and died of a sudden heart attack while in Iceland. She is fondly remembered among Chinese poets for her courageous life and brave poetry.

FLESH

I'm a deep cave
Starved for your wild blaze.
A daylit cloud spread high above your lowlands.
My legs are nimble as a climbing vine.
My breasts, as lucent as lilies.
The breeze off a billowing osmanthus is my face,
My dark hair rippling.
The dew from my eyes
Drenches your desperation.
The sea is bounded in its passion,
But I am boundless,
Stretching in every direction. Nowhere
Will you find flesh more spotless than mine—

Flesh to make you rich—
Flesh you alone may squander.
Peerless, my skin. Incorruptible.
Flowering again
While all around me age after age falls to ruin.

FURTIVE

A black squall blankets the earth.
The stubborn are drenched, worn down. Even
Dreams are slick and choked with moss.

Is meeting out of habit any worse
Than coming clean? I can't let go
Of this clipping lifted from your wife's garden.

Time and again, my voice storms up in a rage,
Weeps back down in tatters.
The daily damage. Still,
My heart harbors a furtive joy.
(Why should I worry?)

I've been careless with your letters, which lie scattered,
Lost. Your name creeps off
Like a plant that has overgrown its pot.

TKS

Yan Li 严力

YAN LI, poet and visual artist, was born in Beijing in 1954 and currently lives between Shanghai and Seattle. He spent ten years in New York from 1985 to 1995. He has been an active avant-garde poet from 1973 to the present time, and one of the earliest spoken-language poets in contemporary China. Largely ignored by the mainstream, he was however rediscovered by Yi Sha and was awarded the Chang-an Achievement Prize in Poetry in 2011.

MEMORIAL

September 11, 2001.
I saw someone on TV jumping
from the World Trade Center—
the scene flashed.
It appeared before me
constantly
and I kept hoping that it was water
he jumped into.
A swimming pool.
A diving competition.
And I could even feel the splash
of water.

Not long ago, the water
really splashed
and wet my shirt
as I suddenly realized:

this could be a way for him
through me
to enter heaven.

9/11/2002
MD, KSK

Yu Jian　于坚

Yu Jian is one of the most prolific poets and writers in contemporary China, born in 1954 in Kunming, Yunnan, southwest China and still lives there. He started writing poetry in college, and in 1985 launched an independent poetry magazine, *Them*, along with the poet Han Dong, which became well known for representing spoken-language poetry in China. Among other awards, he won the Lu Xun Literature Award in 2004.

BEER BOTTLE CAP

Not sure what to call it. A moment ago it was at the end of
   the banquet table,
the guardian of a dark beer, indispensable. It carries a sign of
   its own status.
It means a good mood at sunset, a good head in a glass.
It pops up at the opening of dinner, like a bullfrog
the waiter thinks, as if the rebirth of something among the
   hot food.
The waiter is sorry about his mistake and shifts his attention
   to a toothpick.
He's the last one to have noticed it, ever.
No entry of it in dictionaries. No definition or extended
   meanings.
Even the inferior dishes mean something. Sichuan cuisine.
Even the napkins are used by a general. Roses are in full
   bloom.
The little thing that's popped up is gone up in the air.

The beer factory has never designed the curved line it should
follow when it pops up.
Now it's on the floor with cigarette butts, footprints, bones and
all the dirty things.
They're unrelated to each other, an impromptu mix.
A bottle cap is the worst of all. A cigarette butt reminds people
of a filthy guy.
A bone brings to mind meat and animals. Footprints of a person
and all the paths he has walked through.
A bottle cap is a waste. Its color is nothing. Its shape nothing.
It's beyond all our adjectives.
I wasn't drinking then. I just opened a bottle of beer
so I witnessed its strange leap, it simply disappeared in the air.
I suddenly wanted to "pop" up like the cap, but was unable to.
As the author of a poetry book and a body of sixty kilograms,
all I did was to bend down to pick up this small white rare thing,
its hard toothlike edge lacerating my fingers—
it makes me feel a sharpness unrelated to knives.

1991

READING ROBERT FROST

It isn't easy to read his poems
in a room so close to the street.
In the beginning, I hear knocking on the door,
not sure if I should open it, or not.
Then I'm inside his orchard
hearing long lost sounds.
They jump into the treetops or run into rivers.
I see Frost chewing on russet grass.
I see this old guy proudly strolling by,

one foot on a hoe, his nose hit by the hoe handle.
He's fascinating in his way.
Great wisdom does not seem far off.
I'm going to leave the city tomorrow
and go hiking in the wilderness.

With his little book under my arm
I walk out, and look at the sky.
The path in the backyard
has been covered by snow.

1990
MD, KSK

Yang Lian 杨炼

YANG LIAN was born in Switzerland in 1955 and grew up in Beijing. He was the youngest Misty Poet in the 1970s and 1980s. Since 1988, he has lived in Australia, the US, the UK, and currently in Berlin. His work has been amply translated in English and other languages. He was awarded the Flaiano International Poetry Prize (Italy) in 1999 and the Nonino International Literature Prize (Italy) in 2012. He has traveled frequently in recent years bringing international poets to China and promoting Chinese poetry in the UK and Germany.

A LINE ON THE LIANGZHU JADE CONG

Jade wants to disappear—the carved world in its grip.
Lake-green skin wants to disappear—a strip

Of distant brilliance across the eye—
The line that depicts home also wipes it away

Birds like shark's teeth graze the blue sky—
a precise tender body, so birds and hours fly

you're stitching space—time's needle-tip—
jade dust falls, noise of tsunami, the rip

of pain, of needle—dust falling grit by grit—
a tight network, the skull's shallow dip—

hard carving steeped in softness, *sulci* and *gyri*
hand enters shape, the teardrop's fragrance, now salty

now crispy—beads' brilliance to hold the circle's eye—
exposed target—five thousand years crystalized in a day.

returning only once, you're always about to quit—
like the burnished beauty of the knife's blood slit

with the light in the jade that leaks and silts up—
stone curtains drawn on centuries, time through a gap,

jade at its core is a face-desiring infinity
but infinity has died, as it must always die—

brute natural coral   whiteness   flooding brow-high—
home—the fixed idea, increasing intensity

staring as the tsunami rises in one huge fit—
the first character: one line paints it.

2011

GS

Wang Xiaoni　王小妮

WANG XIAONI (1955–) has been writing since 1974 and gets better with age. With over a dozen volumes of poems, essays and short stories credited to her name, she is regarded as one of the best women poets in the country.

TO THE SUNLIGHT ENTERING MY ROOM

Here you are, just in time to invade my turf.
Half my desk receives your warmth—
inventor of happiness, the tenured professor.
You come only to offer golden comfort,
leave behind ripening fruits, budding flowers,
cotton and grain bursting out—your luster
displays the earth's bright abundance.
But behind all this are sweat,
coughing, gasping, and moldy cracks—
don't think that I haven't seen this.
I refuse to be bathed in you again. Winter shivers;
I don't deserve your light.

2010
MD, KSK

Zhai Yongming　翟永明

ZHAI YONGMING (1955–) is one of the most well-known women poets in China. She started publishing poetry in 1984 and became known for her feminist voice. She has published several collections of poems and essays since then, winning the Zhongkun Poetry Award in 2007 and many national awards.

BIDIS

Xi Chuan handed me a bidi,
the same kind he smoked ten years ago.

A bidi is not a More
but has the same sexy smell
of the lower classes.

Poets smoke bidis
imagining they're getting a taste of the slums.
But actually we are in the embassy zone
with a carpet of green grass outside the windows,
green peacocks strutting around.
Big black crows flap around the chatterboxes
at our roundtable talks.

We feel ashamed—not just of our anemic writing
or writing in Hindi, Thai,
Chinese or Bengali,
or debating on religions or nationalisms.

So many questions have been translated
again and again
like the bidis being smoked by people of all walks of life
who put a bidi to their lips, inhale, and puff
ring after ring of local smells, depoliticized.

2009
MD, KSK

Mo Yan 莫言

MO YAN is a novelist but started writing poetry in recent years. He was born Guan Moye in Shandong in February 1955. He joined the army in 1976, and published his first novel in 1981. He entered a military academy in 1984, and rose to fame in 1986 when publishing another novel, *Red Sorghum*, which was adapted into a film in 1988 that won international awards. In that same year he obtained an MA in literature from Beijing Normal University. He was awarded the Nobel Prize in Literature in 2012 for his work "with hallucinatory realism" that merges with "folk tales, history and the contemporary." Currently he lives between his hometown in Shandong and Beijing and teaches at Beijing Normal University. This poem is from the seven-poem sequence published in the *People's Literature* journal in September 2017.

PAMUK'S STUDY ROOM

—For Orhan Pamuk far away

Stomach tucked in, I enter a narrow elevator
to get to his study room—the guy's hot,
hotter than me back in my home country.
"My name is red."

I've been to many colleagues' studies
but none has such an aura.
It's not really big but holds many books.
The floor creaks, the bookshelves shabby.
A round table by the window, a small chair
by the table. That's where he has afternoon tea—

once you come out to his balcony,
you are really in his study.

The most alluring scene is the sunset at dusk,
a brilliant view of visions:
shadowy islands in front to the left,
lights from a shipyard ahead to the right.
A church in rose color beneath my eyes,
its beautiful dome, a jade pillar pointing to the sky.
Pink seagulls circling around.
Asia on the left, Europe on the right.
A shrine below, a nirvana above.
An ocean lies ahead. Here you can hear
the heartbeat of Istanbul.
Here you can hear two continents
colliding.

Pamuk threatens to throw books by local authors,
age fifty to sixty, out the window—
stupid mediocre with small achievements,
gut feelings lost daily,
male, bald.
He takes the English version of *Red Sorghum*
from the shelf.
I touch my head. In panic.
He smiles: You are not a local.
But in the end he throws my book
from the balcony anyway—
four seagulls catching it just in time.
They carry it like a piece of bread
and drop it on the dome.
Is there a better destiny than
this?

2017
MD, KSK

Liu Xiaobo　刘晓波

LIU XIAOBO (1955–2017) was a literary critic, writer, poet, and human rights activist. He was born in Jilin in December 1955, and went to Jilin University in 1977. While in college, he founded a poetry club with six classmates including Wang Xiaoni who is also in this anthology. He went on to Beijing Normal University for his MA and PhD degrees in literature, where he became a lecturer in 1988. He published extensively while in graduate school. He was a visiting scholar at Columbia University in 1989 when the Tiananmen Students Movement broke out in Beijing. He returned to China to support the movement and was arrested. After he was released from jail in 1991, he lost his teaching job and became a full-time dissident writer. In 2012 when he was in jail for the fourth time, he was awarded the Nobel Peace Prize for his "long and nonviolent struggle for fundamental human rights in China." He died a political prisoner on July 13, 2017 due to liver cancer.

MORNING
—For Xia

Between the gray walls
and a burst of chopping sounds,
morning comes, bundled and sliced,
and vanishes with the paralyzed souls
of the chopped vegetables.

Light and darkness pass through my pupils.
How do I know the difference?

Sitting in rust, I can't tell
if it's the shine on the shackles in the jail
or the natural light of Nature
from outside the walls.
Daylight betrays everything, the splendid sun
stunned.

Morning stretches and stretches in vain.
You are far away—
but not too far to gather the love
of my night.

1997
MD

Ouyang Jianghe   欧阳江河

OUYANG JIANGHE (1956–) began publishing poetry in 1979 and emerged in 1985 as one of the most important Post-Misty Poets. He has also published critical reviews of music and film. From 1993–1997, he lived in the US and currently lives in Beijing as poet-in-residence at Beijing Normal University. He won the Chinese Literature Award from the Southern Media Group in 2011.

FADO

the son's still the same but the mother's changed
the mother still the same but the woman different
there are no women outside of Portugal—

the larynx is still the same but the womb is different
life still the same but it goes beyond life
the same person's before our eyes, but beyond life's coil

the son stuffs himself inside his mother's mouth
orphans himself from God inside his father's body
orphan of the ocean, how can these hot tears keep from
    flowing

the ocean turning around, not a body's turning
a body's martyring and flaying
slapped with an oceanful of water, we leave downcast

the day's the same but not the iteration
O god, my life starts today
but our question is: how to live through another day?

it's still the same old debt but the creditor's already dead
the new bankers are immaculately dressed
with a clap of thunder, they become the world's stepfathers

it's still the same silver coin but all the earth's gold has run dry
psalms and hymns kneel before each other in a reel of leaves
the word, *mute*, and the cries of birds are tracks of wormholes

the ocean stuffs the woman into a microphone
but still can't sing the whole sorrow
still can't hear this loneliness as deep O deep as the sea

unless the ocean endless is bound into a grain of crystal sand
unless the dried bones of man's voice are stripped clean
unless the human heart is sung until deaf and pulpy

the muteness is the same but it's a silent angel singing
the mouth of the enemy and the godsend open together
only to be shut by an orphan's skull

2017
KY

Fado *is a traditional genre of Portuguese songs, meaning* fate. *Men go to sea and women sing to the sea about their fate.*

Sun Wenbo 孙文波

SUN WENBO (1956–) is one of the most distinguished poets from the nonacademic side. Born in Sichuan, southwest China, he served in the army for a few years before working in factories, and then he became a literary editor in the mid 1980s. He was a major poet promoting narrative writing in the 1990s. He lives in Shenzhen at present, editing an independent magazine, *Contemporary Poetry*.

NOTHING TO DO WITH CROWS

First just one, then a flock
flapping their curved wings
before me—darkness sweeping the sky.
I watch as if watching a play unfold, a drama of nature.
A single crow is mystery, a flock of crows is fear.
Humans can't escape
the past, the consciousness—the crows
flying within me: witchcraft, prophecy, forbidden
    awakening.
I sit, limited: I believe what I don't understand,
trust what I don't believe, like a country
built on mistaken foundations constructing a false enemy.
I miss the days of youth, the fence of language
not yet built—only imagining, remembering—
the black crows and white snow opposite but one,
pure beauty, a paradox in paradise—to vanish
was to be eternal—I watch now, the crows become fiction,

flying outside me—they're not really there, circling in
   silence;
they're not really there, dwelling high on the glassy roofs.

2006
MD, NA

Zhang Shuguang　张曙光

Born in 1956 in Heilongjiang, **ZHANG SHUGUANG** was educated there and later worked there as a professor of literature. Along with Xiao Kiayu and Sun Wenbo from Sichuan, he started an independent magazine called *The Nineties* which became influential. Later he became one of the three chief editors for *Chinese Poetry Review* (the other two were Zang Di and Xiao Kaiyu), which folded in 2015. He is also a distinguished translator of Dante.

TO XUEFEI

I can't imagine your face, your body and voice
swallowed up by the streets of New York,
your head tilted to one side, your neck unable to hold the
      weight of ideas.
I can tell it's you from a distance.
You are so clumsy
driving across Brandeis, your wife is working
making souvenirs, missing your son
in China. Why you choose this damned career
as a poet, I don't know. Your father curses you. You never
care about him. And I don't know him but he
writes in a cursive way like you
since you are his son and you
are in America, and Allen Ginsburg
and John Ashbery
are also there! How I like them. How I like you but
I don't know why

you chose this damned career as a poet.
I try to read your face in dreams. Your face becomes blurry
and strange. I can't imagine how you
eat steak in a restaurant. Perhaps you never went there
or you went there just to be a hard laborer.
If I see you I'll punch you and say Hey Buddy don't lick
your fingers, speak better Chinese, boy,
and I'll drag you
from your wife's angry eyes to City Lights,
San Francisco,
City Lights, my Charlie Chaplin, City lights.

1987
KF, MD

Bai Hua　柏桦

Bai Hua (1956–), born in Sichuan, is one of the prominent figures of the Post-Misty Poets. After a silence of more than a decade, he began writing poetry again in 2007 and won the Rou Gang Poetry Award in the same year. He has also received the Anne Kao Poetry Prize. Currently he teaches at the Southwestern Transportation University, founder of Zhang Zao Poetry Prize.

MARCH IN KARLSTAD, WHERE GOD IS SPEEDING PAST

Early morning, what is the quivering calmness evading?
Karlstad! Tall gods and goddesses flash by
speeding . . . before the City Hotel
Empty streets; frozen lake, European block houses with
  no one . . .

As a heart from 2011 walks on a 1797 stone bridge
the nerves of the naked birch tree terrify me

In March, a textile factory springs out of the forest
Klässbols!
Please! Furiously stir the art of afternoon. In harmony
yet another god speeds past—

I see a Chinese scientist holding an iPhone
crossing the Swedish sky like a falling star

FSL

Tong Wei　童蔚

TONG WEI (1956–), daughter of Zheng Min, was born in Beijing and has been publishing poetry since 1983. She participated in international poetry festivals in the 1990s. Her poems have appeared in many important anthologies in China. She also writes essays and has worked as a literary editor for *China's Woman Daily* for twenty years.

DREAMING ABOUT TIGERS

You—have you ever seen tigers,
stone-hearted tigers, shredding white sheets, vicious,
in a pack yet solitary. Books don't discuss this.

I see tigers behind trees, ripping strips of sheet.
I recall the tigers' warnings
and I know something transpired on earth,
but they won't reveal what.
When they feel an urge in their bones
they rip into each other,
their bones collide chaotically.
The strips are tiger stripes drawn by visionary artists.
Each stroke spurs vertigo,
each stroke is a clump of tiger stripes
the tigers have stripped from each other.
The entire street is snagged in a tiger's mouth
so that you have to rush out through its teeth
to compete amidst the gore
for ultimate immortality.

2011
RG, MD

Wang Jiaxin　王家新

WANG JIAXIN (1957–) was born in Danjiangkou, Hubei Province, central China, and graduated from Wuhan University in 1982. He was one of the most important poets in the Third Generation and he promoted Intellectual Writing in the 1990s. He is currently a professor of literature at Renmin University in Beijing. His poetry and his translation work have been widely published. He won numerous awards in China including the Translation Award of Book Trade in 2017.

DIARY

He starts at the lush oak tree,
making small circles on the lawn to a larger
circle. I listen to the gardener mowing, sniff
the grass, the freshness of the cutting,
I breathe in, and enter another garden
of my imagination where the grass is swallowing
the white marble carvings on the bench—
waves of grass, like death caressing me
with human fingers.

I wake up, and see an abandoned mower.
It's cold. Things around me are submitting to something
    colder.
The oak tree bursting out, the gardener
at rest, eternally. It starts snowing
from my pen—it will not fill the garden

but fills my throat. This white death, the reincarnation of
   seasons
of a larger death, I love the
choking white snow, the thrill of loss. I recall
the last green breath of grass . . .

1992
MD

Liao Yiwu　廖亦武

LIAO YIWU, born in Sichuan in 1958, became known as a poet through-out China in the 1980s, but later decided to be an underground writer. From 1990 to 1994 he was imprisoned as a result of the long poem "Massacre" he wrote in June, 1989. He left China in 2010 and has been living in Berlin as a performing artist in exile. He was a fellow at DAAD in 2012 and won the Peace Prize of the German Book Trade in 2012.

FOR MY DAUGHTER

Let me sit here in this corner,
an imaginary cell for praying,
my hands handcuffed behind me
making a sign of the cross
for you, Miao Miao, my daughter,

little thing that probes and peeks—
I eat you from the dust every day.
The cement sunroof splits: a moon.
I see you on that mountain,
foggy. I see you in a saddle.

1991
MD

RHETORIC

I say do not get close to these poems. Stones. Sun.
Water. Do not touch. This man-made sky. You want to
control, your cowardly hands. Each word is skin and
it grows. Heals itself, the masterpiece of the earth, the
masterpiece decays before becoming the masterpiece.
Masterpiece, thin. If you recite a line of poetry, you are
tearing a piece of silk, you are ripping off the skin. See:
the wound swells, diffuses, rots idols alive. Beauty is
thin as always—in paper, in snow, in feathers, silk, Wei
Li and Fei Fei, these names, thin. Control, you want.
Possession, you want. Possess nothing, idiots. Behind
the decay of beauty is emptiness, openness, loneliness.
Beauty is open—dazzling, charmingly empty. And you,
idiots, want to take control of your hands I say.

MD, KF

Song Lin　宋琳

SONG LIN (1959–) was born in Fujian and went to college in Shanghai. He has lived in Paris, Singapore, Buenos Aires, and Beijing, and has now settled down in Yunnan province, China. He has been the poetry editor for Bei Dao's *Today* journal since 1992. Currently he coedits *Poetry Reading Quarterly* with Pan Xichen. He has published five collections of poetry and was awarded the first Dong Dangzi prize in China in 2014.

ENCOUNTERING SNOW AT RED SNAIL TEMPLE

Snow, coming down aimlessly,
giddy, eternal spell,
or a stage for dreams;
muddled footprints go on without end.
On the stairways to the Little Sky Gate,
the Buddhist pilgrims climb
carrying with them another year of grief.

Stranded beside unmarked rocks,
discarded straw sandals
share the quiet with the snow.

O! Impetuous men
looking back at the path they trekked
in the pine woods on the mountainside
as the village smoke
melts away the first snow.

The flower of your secret wishes
drifts down in circles
before the Buddha statue.

The wondrous realm is beyond words
as is the rapture of Sun greeting snow.
The bell tolls, again and again,
beating against the silence of the mountains.

2005
DL, KSK

Xiao Kaiyu   萧开愚

XIAO KAIYU was born in 1960 in a village in Zhongjiang County, Sichuan Province. He studied Chinese medicine in college. Along with Zhang Shuguang and Sun Wenbo, he promoted narrative poetry in the 1990s as against the lofty lyricism in the 1980s. He lived in Berlin for six years, and currently teaches literature in Shanghai and Henan, China.

MAO ZEDONG

By cutting off excessive colors and shapes
the Great Man makes the content clear.
He prefers the silver of clouds—the azure blue
of sea—the grandeur of things
in tidy appearance. He loves this kind of a country.

The sun is fixed like a badge on the forehead
above an ocean of people.
Forged in steel, a vast reality
weaves the infinite into a finite but illusive square
built around the tower, not made of gold but clay.

Newspapers cheer the ideal victory,
the unruly tide rises.
A hurricane of a hundred million hearts lifts the drooping
   banners,
and sweeping waves sail the seawater to new heights.
The sea holds only wrecks and submarines.

He lies in his study, a converted swimming pool
full of ancient books, staring into the air,
speaking short cryptic phrases, in a raspy voice, riddled
with indecipherable meanings, a soldier's language
from an unseen battlefield—who can understand him?

1987
MD, NA

Lü De'an　吕德安

LÜ DE'AN (1960–) was born in a small town in Fujian, southeast coast of China and started writing poetry in the late 1970s. He lived in New York City from 1991 to 1994 as an artist and returned to China in 1995. He kept a low profile until his third collection of poetry came out in 2010 and received nationwide recognition.

NIGHT AT OCEAN CORNER, AND WOMEN

Ocean Corner, Ocean Corner,
a fishing village
in the shape of a fisherman's footprint,
immerses in water like a fan spreading its spikes.
A black shirt with sparkling stars
blows across
when night falls. And here

people go to sleep early, with salty air outside
the windows. Nearby, evening lights
on fishing boats scatter, a sign of
nets down in the ocean—they've waited
a thousand years for the fish.
Night is dark. Children cry as if there're no parents
around—they're in deep dreams.
Children cry. But it's time

to go to sleep. Children get quiet. So do the small hours
of deep night at Ocean Corner. Everyone sinks into
happiness with a bubbling smile
and this is the most beautiful moment—
no voices by the men's side gently pushing:
"Time to go to sea."

1979

THE ROOF GUYS

But they're local—the roof guys
of roof guys who really know
roofs. They move
in the same fashion
with the same caution. When they walk on the roofs
even the clay tiles crack
in the same direction.
They are careful but still
you can hear the
creaking.
Open one up—dust rises
like tiny insects
resurrected. Every being lives
for the same purpose—
to be opened.

Roof guys come and go
replacing each other's faces.
At sunset, they disappear.
But this time they remain—as our specimens,

awkwardly moving, one by one
on the roofs.
Looking toward them, you find them gone,
and yet they seem to have stayed the night,
or an entire age.

1987
MD

Mo Fei 莫非

MO FEI, a poet and botanic photographer, has been publishing poems with photographs on his popular blog. Born in Beijing in 1961, he started publishing poetry in the 1970s, and became one of the Third Road Poets during the conflicts between the spoken language poets and intellectual writing poets. He is retired from his daytime job as a botanic specialist and currently lives in Dali, Yunnan, southwest China.

SOME FLOATING TIME IN LIGHT—FOR YOU

Some days floating in light for you, some water for the trees,
some gentle wind for the new moon. Some whispering for
  the words,

the rest are evening lights for the clouds and the fairies.
Some plums for the twigs and branches, some rivers

for the wells. Some jade for the roofs and eaves.
Some windows for the walls, some walls for the ears.

Some beans around the house back and front, some rain
for the season. Some labor for those who don't work,

some ladders up and down for toon leaves and persimmons.
Some cats calling, some trespassing in the spring for a next
  life

Some pains for growing, some pains for blooming.
Some birds for the evenings and some evenings for the
songs.

2010
MD

Han Dong 韩东

HAN DONG is a well-known poet and novelist in China. Born in 1961 in Nanjing, he graduated from Shandong University in 1982 with a degree in philosophy. He taught in Xi-an for a while and moved back to Nanjing. In 1985, he launched an independent poetry journal *Them* with Yu Jian and promoted spoken-language poetry. He has published several books of poetry and novels, and started making independent films in 2016.

MOUNTAIN PEOPLE

When he was little, he asked his father
"What's over the mountain."
"Mountains," his father said.
"What's over the mountains?"
"Mountains, more mountains."
He fell silent, looking into the distance.
Mountains made him tired for the first time.

He thought he could never get out of the mountains
in this life. The sea was there, but far away.
He would only live a few decades
and before reaching the sea
he would have died in the mountains
halfway there.

So why not take the better half along, he thought.
His better-half wife would bear him a son

and his son would have grown up
when he died.
And his son would have a wife
and a son and his son's son
would have a son too.

He doesn't think any more.
Even the "son" makes him tired.
He only regrets
his ancestors didn't think like him.
Or he would have been the one to see the sea.

1982
MD, KSK

Chen Dongdong　陈东东

CHEN DONGDONG, born in Shanghai in 1961, was one of the Third Generation in China that rose in the 1980s trying to bypass the Misty Poets such as Bei Dao. Poets of the Third Generation were not interested in the political lyricism that prevailed in the Misty poetry as well as in the mainstream poetry, nor did they care about the dominant realistic aesthetics. Zhang Zao, Bai Hua and Chen Dongong are known today for their experiment in the 1980s when they were trying to revive the classical language. They are in the New Poetry (free verse) camp but they favor the subtleties of Chinese and the classical tone as against the plainspoken language. In the 1990s, Chen Dongdong was one of the "intellectual writing" poets along with Xi Chuan, Ouyang Jianghe, and Wang Jiaxin. He currently lives in the suburb of Shenzhen, southern China.

LIGHT UP

Light up an oil lamp in the rocks so they can see
the sea. Let them see
the sea and the antique fish.
See the light too,
a lamp held high on the hill.

Light up a lamp in the streams so they can see
the living fish. Let them see
the fish and the silent sea.
See the sunset as well,
a firebird flying up from the trees.

Light up all the lamps. When I block the north wind
with my hands and stand between two canyons,
I think they will all gather around me
and see I speak a language
like a lamp.

1985
MD

Jidi Majia　吉狄马加

JIDI MAJIA is an ethnic Yi-Nuosu poet, born in 1961 in Sichuan. His first collection of poems, *Song of Love*, won the National Poetry Prize in 1986, followed by the publication of over a dozen books of poems and essays. His work has been translated into many languages and he has been awarded numerous international prizes including the Sholokhov Memorial Medal for Literature in 2006 from the Russian Writers' Association, a Certificate for Outstanding Contributions in Poetry from the Bulgarian Writers Association in 2006, and the HOMER Medal of Poetry and Art in 2016. He used to be the vice governor of Qinghai Province and is now deputy director of the National Writers Association and founder of Qinghai Lake Poetry Festival, Xichang Literary Week and Chengdu Literary Week.

WHEN DEATH IS NEAR

"You have become an orphan on this day,"
I'm told—no mercy for how I'm overwhelmed.
When the white with darkness was overlaid,
Mother passed into another realm.

Don't question what an orphan knows of pain.
When mother dies you understand *lonely*
and *helpless*. Till the boulder drowned in waves,
throughout my life I leaned on mother only.

When death arrives, curses waste their meaning.
Death called your name out in his mother tongue:
Nizi Guogezhuoshi, mount your

white horse that waits at the gate, go toward
the hill above the town, where in colors gleaming
and gravely weeping, are your sisters who died young.

2016
From "Twenty Sonnets for My Mother"
TB, MD

Luo Yihe　骆一禾

LUO YIHE (1961–1989) was the first to discover Hai Zi's talent as a poet in the early 1980s who became a legendary figure after committing suicide in 1989. Luo was born in Beijing in 1961. After graduation from Beijing University, he became a literary editor with the *October* monthly in Beijing and won the prize of Outstanding Editor twice. He started publishing poetry in 1983 and died at age twenty-eight: he joined the hunger strike at Tiananmen (the Square of Heavenly Peace Gate) on May 13 and died on May 31, the first poet who died because of supporting the 1989 Students Movement. "Heaven" and "square" refer to the location where the 1989 Students Movement took place.

SPLENDID, SUPPRESSED

This year's spring storms
will seize us.
Everything grows around Heaven,
and even Heaven itself is growing
like a lush pine-forest
growing something called "inseparable."
It leaves the square to be cleaned in the autumn.
Crops will get squandered on the ground.
I will not harvest them—the square as witness, so immense
as if all seasons are here.
Autumn will sing, its face lit by our hometown lights:
the spring storms
that will never let us go on easily—never this year.

May 10, 1989
MD

Liu Xia 刘霞

LIU XIA (1961–) is a Chinese poet and fiction writer, widow of the Nobel Peace Laureate Liu Xiaobo. She published short stories in the 1980s and has been writing poetry since 1982. She is also an artist with over 300 paintings and several series of black-and-white photographs. Her first book of poetry in English translation, *Empty Chairs* (Graywolf Press, 2015), was selected by the *Washington Independent Review of Books* as one of the best books in 2015 and was a finalist of the Best Translated Book Award in 2016. She won the Poetry Award from *DJS-Poetry East West* in 2014.

ROAD TO DARKNESS
—*For Xiaobo*

Sooner or later you will leave
me one day
and take the road to darkness
alone.

I pray for the moment to reappear
so I can see it better,
as if from memory.
I wish that I, astonished, could glow, my body
in full bloom of light for you.

But I couldn't have made it
except by clenching my fists, not letting

the strength,
not even a little bit of it, slip
through my fingers.

2010

MD

FRAGMENT NO. 8

I often look at the light
from death
and feel warm, then loss
when I have to leave the page.
I want to be in light.

My strength, worked for years,
has become dust. A tree
can be destroyed
by lightning,
which ends the thinking.

For me the future is
a closed window
where night has no end
and nightmares can't be lifted.

I want to be in light.

2011

MD, JS

Zhang Zao 张枣

ZHANG ZAO (1962–2010), born in Hunan, made his name as a poet while a student in Sichuan. He went to Germany in 1986 and became the poetry editor of Bei Dao's *Jintian* journal in the 1990s. He spent his last five years teaching in China and died of lung cancer. *Plum* (梅) in this poem is a typical ancient image and it resembles *regret* (悔) in shape and in sound. It's a popular poem and what general readers find interesting is the Emperor, something that has disappeared since the Qing Dynasty ended in 1911. Zhang Zao is remembered for his experiment in language and subject matters in poetry.

MIRROR

Plum flowers fall whenever regret awakes—
as in watching her swim to the other shore
or climb a pinewood ladder.
Dangerous things are beautiful;
it's better to see that she returns on horseback,
her face warm,
abashed, her head lowered, responding to the Emperor.
A mirror awaits her, as always,
allowing her to sit inside it, in her usual place,
and gaze out the window—regrets awaken all the plum
flowers
as they fall, like egrets, over the South Hills.

1984
MD

Qing Ping 清平

QING PING (pen name for Wang Qingping, 1962–) is a well-respected poetry editor in Beijing. He has been working at the People's Literature Publishing House since he graduated from Beijing University in 1983. He has published two books of poetry and is known for editing the prestigious *Blue Stars Poetry Series*, and the bilingual edition *Push Open the Window: Contemporary Poetry from China* (Copper Canyon Press, 2011).

TONGHUI RIVER IN BEIJING

I arrive at this mysterious source today,
or more likely the end of a river. It's dark,
quiet, unaware of me.
I see it, or it sees me and observes me.
Deep in the winter, someone like me,
having been to Spring already,
looks at the river, too early in time.

The river runs long, or I've walked long,
but not strenuously.
It's only part of it: it extends by itself
without me, like a spider web
working hard, persistently.
It keeps going, unable to retract. There
has to be something ahead.
I turn around, as if the road I've occupied

turns away from me and from the river that tries
to take it along. Who takes who?
The desire to possess is uncontrollable.
The river makes a turn, free from all.

1993
MD

Wang Yin 王寅

WANG YIN was born in 1962 in Shanghai, a poet, journalist, and photographer. He started publishing poetry in 1983 and was one of the most important poets from the Third Generation. Currently he is a reporter for the *Southern Weekly*. He hosts a series of international readings in Shanghai called Poetry Comes to the Museum.

REMEMBERING A CZECH MOVIE BUT NOT ITS NAME

The cobblestone street is wet
So is Prague
A girl around the corner of the park kisses you
You don't even blink your eyes
Later when you face a gun, no blinking of eyes either
A Nazi soldier wears his raincoat inside out
like a shiny leather jacket
A three-wheeled motorcycle goes by
You and your friends stumble
It's still raining
I see raindrops chase each other
on an electric power line
and finally drip down on a cobblestone
I think of you—
my lips move a little
but no one sees

MD

Sen Zi 森子

SEN ZI (1962–) is an artist and journalist. Born in Heilongjiang, he moved to Henan at age sixteen and there studied art in collage. He became an avant-garde poet in the 1980s, and founded an independent magazine, *Front*, in 1991, that helped gain national recognition for many local poets in Henan. At present he works as an editor for a newspaper in Henan. He has been awarded the Liu Li-an Poetry Prize and the 2013 *Poetry East West* Prize.

ON THE YELLOW RIDGE

First, we inquire about the wild appearance
of a rose-wife
when the leopard is taking a nap in our bodies.

We gather around a bonfire one night,
under a low constellation, our lips
sense the listening enemies.
The leopard wakes up and walks to the village
knocking on the wrong door: nobody's there, just old clothes
on the bed.

In fact, there is no bed, only the imagination of creatures
with four feet.
A savage mountain man looks into the well and tries to fish
for his own reflection. The wall without a door
opens itself.

We walk in. The mountain man has been waiting
for the encounter—he jumps on you, and stabs your chest.
Pieces of yellow clothes scatter on the floor.
What sounds impossible spreads through poems. But
we've missed the wild rose-wife.
So we wait for opportunities with optimism.
But disappointment seems to be replacing hope.
After all, we've been looking for what's not
in our bodies.

2013
MD, KSK

Xi Chuan 西川

Xi Chuan (penname of Liu Jun) was born in Jiangsu in 1963 but grew up in Beijing and graduated from Beijing University with a major in English Literature. He started writing poetry in the early 1980s and became well known as one of the Post-Misty Poets in the intellectual writing group. He has won many awards including the People's Literature Award (1994) and the Lu Xun Literature Award (2001).

ACROSS THE RIVER

Across the river
a fire is burning
A fire
burns May
and burns August

When the ash tree blooms, a professor bows to her
Age spots on his face
When the ash flowers fall, a well-mannered young man
of a noble family waves to her and smiles

But she only burns on the other side of the river
like a red coral glittering underwater
like a red straw hat blown away by a strong wind

Yesterday I saw her, she was still watching the sky
but today she lowers her head, watching the river flow

If it's a cloudy or rainy day, what would she be doing
on the other side of the river—her flames will not cease

A poet sees her
A farmer sees her
A Marxist sees her
She's across the river, burning
She burns through May
She burns through August

A PORTRAIT OF NERUDA

Often at the end of everything
with only music floating like dusk
I start to notice
his portrait hanging on the wall.
Mountains and wild foxes sweep over.
Pablo Neruda starts to
observe the room.
It's full of dust and mottos
and I sit over there
leafing through the books and newspapers
chatting with friends.
A hundred times the sun comes in
and I always miss the moment
yet Pablo
is always like a shadow
with his fat chin pressed down
searching for the young master
of this room.
When I fall asleep but can't dream of

surfing boards and summers
he writes the poems for me
and quietly
places them on my dirty table.

MD

Li Yawei 李亚伟

LI YAWEI rose to fame in the 1980s for his anti-cultural poetry influenced by the American Beat Generation. Born in Chongqing in 1963, he was founder of the well-known Macho group, and he was also included in the first issue of the *Not Not* journal by another group of avant-garde poets. After a break in writing (due to involvement in the publishing business), he is back to the poetry scene with a strong lyrical voice.

LYRICAL SONGS FOR THE RIVER WEST CORRIDOR

1.

The gigantic families of the River West Corridor live
in their glorious past. The world is very old but
some permanent laborers are still laboring outside of
    history.
The three brothers of Wang still follow their fate, their
    families
raking their ancestors' property on the moon.

Noble blood takes turns performing its circulating
duties. The huge dynasties have been eaten by politics
and pushed into a cricket account.
Memorial bells ring and ring again, disappearing
into outer space.

I only live in part of my life. What is it to be living,
what is it to be dead, I don't know.
Sometimes I live outside my life
bound by the national interest.

first poem of a sequence
MD, KSK

Li Yuansheng　李元胜

Li Yuansheng (1963–), from Sichuan, is a poet, novelist, journalist, and ecological photographer. He went to college for engineering but became a poet. He started publishing poetry in 1981, and founded the *Boundaries* in 1999, the first poetry website in China. He was deputy director of the Chongqing Publishing Group until he retired a few years ago to become a full-time writer. He won the Lu Xun Literature Award in 2014 and lives between Chongqing and Yunnan.

SOME PEOPLE WALK TOO FAST

Some people walk too fast
and get ahead of themselves sometimes,
their faces blurred
with the color of future illusions
speeded up by the speed itself.

Likewise, some people walk too slow
and fall behind themselves sometimes.
They are but their own shadows,
with a past full of cracks. They even become
the trash they've always wanted
secretly to get rid of.

Those sitting under the trees
don't happen to be exactly themselves.
Sometimes they sit on their left,

sometimes on their right.
Luckily, on the whole, they sit not too far
from their true selves.

MD

Yang Xiaobin　杨小滨

YANG XIAOBIN was born in Shanghai in 1963, holds a PhD from Yale, taught at the University of Mississippi, and currently works as a research fellow at the Academia Sinica in Taipei. He has published several books of poetry and poetry criticism. He won the First Poetry Book Prize in Taiwan and has served as a jury member for international literary committees. His abstract photography along with abstract poetry titled "Palimpsest and Trace: Post-Photographism" has been exhibited in Taipei, Shanghai and Beijing.

THE CLAY POT IN TENNESSEE

I brought a Chinese clay pot to Tennessee,
smashed it, and the aroma of fish soup bloomed,
lifting and wafting like flower petals in the spring air
before settling onto the muddy pond of a grocery store.

All the catfish grinned. So happy, they almost devoted
themselves to the broken pieces—with another pot of noodle soup,
their kisses still would only reach the lady-boss's rosy cheeks
with a seal of the Overseas Chinese Association.

An unpatriotic clay pot cannot grow into a mushroom cloud,
nor has the time to nurture a nation's fine taste through small talk.
I lie down in Tennessee, kneading the fish lips that are licking the clay,
as if only through breaking can a pot's fragrance become strong.

2005
MD, NA

Zhang Qinghua　张清华

ZHANG QINGHUA was born Shandong in 1963. He was a professor of Chinese literature in Shandong but relocated to Beijing Normal University in 2005. He is a poet and literary critic, and executive director of the International Writing Center at Beijing Normal University. He won the Critics Award of the annual Chinese Literature Awards from the Southern Media Group in 2010.

BREEZE BLOWS BY

great-grandmother in her afternoon shade
swinging her palm leaf fan
her loose breasts sag
like late-autumn gourds

breeze blows by

great-grandfather beneath the eaves weaves his basket
humming his hackneyed tune
that old, off-key thing, like a late-summer cricket
on the road of sweethearts

breeze blows by

a yellowing magazine curled on a cold bench
the reading glasses rest on one arm

a cigarette still trailing smoke
like memory's twilight, half-bright, half-gray

breeze blows by . . .

2003
GP

Zhou Qingrong　周庆荣

Zhou Qingrong (1963–) was born in northern Jiangsu and attended Suzhou University. After graduate study in International Cultural Exchanges at Beijing University in 1993, he has been working in Beijing. Author of five volumes of prose poems including *Love is a Moon Tree* and *Us*. He is the chief editor of *Grand Poetry*.

HISTORY OF CHINA IN NUMBERS

Five thousand years—two thousand years of legends, three thousand years of records.

Ten thousand harvests—how many people and animals did they feed?

On 18,025,000 dawns the roosters crowed—to whom did dogs bark for 20,000 seasons?

One thousand years of wars of secession, a thousand years of wars of union, and a thousand years of fragmenting confederation. Two thousand years of reluctant fealty to temples, waving different flags, chanting different scriptures. Given one thousand years of true unity, five hundred would be taken by black nights. In the remaining five hundred years of brilliant days, how many hearts were scarred by unrecorded rainy days?

How many mysterious archives were sealed up by five hundred years of black nights? How many heroes were buried in earth? How many monuments were built by time for them? And where are the monuments? Sunshine tears through the clouds—how many monuments fall outside the territory of nine million and six hundred thousand square kilometers?

What I also want to calculate is: In these five thousand years how many days were earmarked for dreaming, how many days for justice and joy?

The numbers are certain. Five thousand years of endurance, five thousand years of living, five thousand for the great and the mean, and five thousand years of hope.

Love for five thousand years and loathing for five thousand years. Helpless love of this land for five thousand years. Violence, suffering, vile people achieving vast ambitions I refuse to count. The human heart is greater than five thousand years.

MC, TB

Pan Xichen 潘洗尘

PAN XICHEN (1963–) emerged in the 1980s as a campus poet and won many awards. After twenty years as an entrepreneur in the advertising business, he returned to poetry in 2007 and has maintained a high profile by editing many journals. He founded his own independent journal *Poetry Reading Quarterly* in 2009. He lives between his hometown Harbin and his new home in Dali, Yunnan.

WHEN THE SUN RISES IT DOESN'T KNOW I'M DEPRESSED

Day breaks.
Trees witness the falling of leaves.
Wind sees the dust.
Some people go to work, punching the time clock.
Some people go begging.
Some people stare at others
who are staring back.
This drama repeats itself.
I look worried, my face a vegetable green.
A bad guy.
Broad daylight
isn't my stage.
I must go to sleep.
When the sun goes down I'll wake up.
The props left behind
will be swamped by the night.
Plants and animals
with persecution phobias

are taking a deep breath with me.
I hear their conversations
but will not relay them to humankind.
Night is so quiet and solemn.
Wind takes the trouble to collect soft breathing
and evil snoring.
All I do is put them into catalogs,
which appears so meaningless
but I enjoy doing it endlessly.
Day breaks again
undetected.
When the sun rises it doesn't know
how depressed I am.

2016
MD, KSK

Hai Zi 海子

HAI ZI (1964–1989) is the pen name of Zha Haisheng, one of the most gifted poets in the 1980s. He became a legendary figure after he committed suicide by lying on a train track in March 1989. Some of his poems have become popular and are taught in middle schools.

FROM WHICH SHOE WILL I WAKE UP TOMORROW?

I think I have been careful enough.
I have exactly ten toes,
ten fingers.
I cried a few times when born
and people will drop a few tears when I'm dead.
I quietly
bring myself along, a package,
and quietly open it
even though I don't like myself.

I sit on earth at dusk,
which doesn't mean I will disappear
from earth at night. In the morning
the same planet lies beneath my ass,
solid and durable.
Hello you old never-dying earth.

Or I should simply be a twig.
I used to sleep in a dark shell,
my head as my frontier.

A pear—
before I took a shape,
I was a white flower feeling the cold and warmth.

Or my head is but a cat
placed on my shoulders.
The woman Lotus Moon who created me is gone.
Sunshine shines on big and small cats.
My breathing proves that
the leaves are fluttering.

I can't give up happiness.
Or on the contrary
I live for pain,
half buried.
I come to the village or the mountains.
I stare at the people—alas the yellow earth is
fertile with flourishing populations.

1985
MD, KSK

Zang Di 臧棣

Born in Beijing in 1964, **ZANG DI** (pen name of Zang Li) started writing poetry in 1982, and is currently teaching poetry at Beijing University. He is one of the most original and prolific poets in China, winning many national literary awards such as the Critic of the Year (2005), Ten Best Young Poets (2005), Ten Best Poets (2006), Ten Best Critics (2007), and Chinese Literature Award from the Southern Media Group (2009).

READING TSANGYANG GYATSO, A SERIES

The Tibetan girls I saw in my childhood
at a Sichuan Fair, far and remote,
have grown into beautiful women in your poems.
You write as if the world can do nothing about them.
Or, time can do nothing about them.
But if you don't write poetry, you can't recognize in yourself
the highest king of the snow kingdom.
Beautiful women are gods, of course.
There is no other way to begin but to begin from the
    beginning.
This is different from whether God is foolish or not.
The women are their own gods but they don't know it.
Or, they are our gods
more than their own. 1987, I was 23, getting dumped
out of the blue
was like being hit by an avalanche.
You have been 23, but the difference is: I have survived it

while you were murdered.
And we have been separated by two hundred years of solitude.
Over the years I approach you as if walking
in your poetry to walk back to myself
quietly. 1989, I was 25,
you were 22, the shadow of the red religion was bluer
than the blue water of Lhasa. 1996, I was 32,
you were 19, but how can a voice be independent
only in snow-capped mountains? 2005, I was 41
and you were 17,
once a rebellious spirit jammed with gems, the moon
became the back door
to any place we wanted to enter. 2014, I am 50
and you are 15, as simple as that. But how is it that
your ambivalence, in a soft shell, has become
my secret and mine alone?

2014
MD

FLYING ASSOCIATION

Between Celan and Amichai there is a Du Fu.
We should drill a well and draw him up,
carve out time to listen to the voice from underground.
Between Amichai and Tranströmer, there is a Wang Wei.
We should dig a hole in the green hill to wake him up
from the sleeping realm of snakes.
Between Celan and Tranströmer, there is a Li Shangyin.
We should drill through the stunned stone,
use thousand-year-old guano to slowly bake his shadow
into a loaf of bread.

Between Amichai and Ted Hughes, there is a Jiang Kui.
We should pull him out of that tree,
put him in a basket, and with a pulley and rope
haul him up to the treetop. There,
the basket becomes a bird's nest, as if we've wandered
into an age when both men and birds try to fly.

2014
MD, NA

Song Wei　宋炜

SONG WEI (1964–) was born in Muchuan, Sichuan Province. He started publishing poems in the early 1980s and was cofounder of the Holistic Poetry group in Chengdu from 1984 to 1989. For many years he remained a hermit until poets and critics rediscovered him and highly praised his work. He was awarded the first Hu Shi Poetry Prize by *DJS-Poetry East West* in 2016.

POEM OF THE BODY

—In mid-spring of the year of wood, I posted myself on the back hill of Red Silk Clouds, meditating. This poem came to me during the meditation.

Tomb-Sweeping Day is over, but the body is still feasting.
Internal organs open like a grocery store: welcome guests.
Guests are the wind, master is the air: they interchange.
Liver is the God on duty today, his hangover
finally over. A sudden epiphany in the eye:
eucommia trees and pears are not trees but medicine and
　　fruit.
To all of these I turn a deaf ear.
I'm not surprised that the organ vessels swept by the airflow
release a dim light.
In between, the lung is so simple. It exhales a crude breath,
and gets self-refreshed repeatedly.
Let the dust settle at the tailbone. Leaves emit a
clapping sound, an echo of their hunger?

Are there hungry intestines hiding in my bulging belly?
Are my hungry intestines carrying waste matter?
Look, it's more than a fart. My pee and golden shit
are food resurrected (they left me and found their way out.)
Stomach is yellow earth shaped into a device
but empty: between the holes, gods of the internal organs
are leaving one by one. In this sparse interior,
even the careful thoughts, or seasonal ideas,
are nothing but small confusions, at most the internal drafts
of a poem. So a bird lands on my head to shit.
The bird thinks I'm transfixed like a wooden chicken,
paying no attention to whatsoever's beautiful around me.
No lush heart. Even my lusty bladder is at rest.
Not even a threat to myself.

SMALL NOTES IN MY OLD AGE

I return to the village and see lots of red peppers
sunbathing on the threshing floor with me,
giving warmth to the summer.
I put my hands to my eyebrow to make an arbor
as if installing an air conditioner in front of my eyes.
In fact, my forehead and my neck are making salt.
Lots of salt. Look, we've made this summer so salty!
And I'm not hospitable enough to myself, otherwise
why should I bring myself this full cup of liquor?
Yes, because I've finally had half of it.
As an antique holistic idealist, I demand everything be complete
including remnants of clouds, embers and death.
However, I can accept what's second best: no old age.
Too many people give up the rest of their lives to be a martyr.
One life is too short to accommodate, might as well leave.

I am so extreme. I either fly up to eat people, or dive
into the sea to watch the stars – the sky collapses,
sea water overflowing. If my old age coincides with this earth,
why aren't we doomed on the same day? If the earth can't wait
for my urgent but sweet deadline, I will say to the world:
Come sooner!

MD, KSK

Zhao Ye　赵野

ZHAO YE (1964–) was originally from Sichuan currently lives in Yunnan. He has a BA in English from the Sichuan University. Along with his fellow poets, he co-launched the Third Generation poetry movement in 1982 and edited the *Third Generation* magazine. He has published several books of poetry, been translated into a few languages, including a German edition *Zurück in die Gärten* published in 2000. He has won the Poetry prize from *The Writers* journal, and Poet of the Year Award from the Heavenly Question Festival.

YELLOW SPARROW ON A FLAGPOLE

The same air moves around us.
It's startling when my index finger
and even my name blaze in the season.
It's the third century, with rusty lumber and slumbering.
A phoenix gently stretches its wide wings
in front of my eyes. Yangtze River flows upward.
I hurry to the river side. Where is the hero?
Who can stop plants from migrating?
Or hold back the pain of rhetoric?
Change my role. Let others replace me.
Let him ride on thin ice. Let me face
the mountain range and stream out my crying.
The rest of my life—I can only hold on to memories.
I know I will die in laziness, having a good view or wine.
Might as well be a yellow sparrow like the one that's
observing me, not a bad view for a beloved one.

MD

Mo Mo　默默

Mo Mo (1964–) is cofounder of the poetry school *Sa Jiao*, which means behaving like a spoiled child or a man moaning like a woman. He says it means "gentle resistance." A whimper, not a bang. He cofounded the school and its journal in 1985 in Shanghai and made it known nationwide by organizing a series of events and by being jailed in 1986 for his long poem "Growing up in China". A legendary figure but hardly known outside China.

A SUPPLEMENTAL EPITAPH FOR GOD

All is dear: dear thought, dear cold,
dear wound, dear vomiting, dear who?
All is dear: dear evening, dear dream,
dear wild dogs, dear leader, dear who?
All is dear: dear eyelashes, dear fate,
dear hero, dear dead trees, dear mountains and waters,
dear who?
All is dear: dear liar, dear memory,
dear birthday, dear bathroom, dear emperor,
dear who?
All can be dear: dear anger, dear fear,
dear betrayal, dear melancholy, dear accident,
dear madness, dear punishment, dear vigilance—
all can be dear: dear desire, dear flickering,
dear silence, dear Pop-, dear star,
dear wings, dear ice, dear whirlpools—
all can be dear: dear olive trees, dear bullet rai-
n, dear United Nations, dear existentialism, dear

refrigerators, dear day and night, dear weak,
dear fleeing from famine, dear cruel-
ty, all can be dear: dear Mayan, dear Bohemian
tricks, dear peace above the Eternal Peace Avenue, dear
   human rights
declaration, dear noise, dear slavery, dear brother
Columbia, dear opium war, dear Challenger cra-
sh, dear history, dear nothingness
all can be dear: dear 1990, dear
kiss, dear hard to separate, dear die in heaven, dear
tears in voice, dear cliff, dear fall,
dear destiny
all is dear that can be dear,
dear secret, dear graveyard.

MD, KSK

Na Ye　娜夜

NA YE is an ethnic Manchu poet in China. Born in 1964, she has spent most of her life in the wild west of Lanzhou as a journalist but recently moved to Chongqing City in central China. With several collections of poetry published, she has won both of the two major awards for poetry in China: the People's Literature Award and the Lu Xun Literature Award.

LIFE

I've cherished you
as a brown bonbon from my childhood.
I licked it and immediately wrapped it up.
One more lick . . .
Slowly I licked it, more and more slowly
and wrapped it up more and more quickly.
Now there's only me with the plastic wrapper.
I should not say it aloud what saddens me.

JOY

How trustworthy this old flame,
these potatoes with fresh mud, these cabbages,
the steam from the hot bread,
the frost on the radishes.

Now, I'm no longer a stranger
to myself,
nor is life elsewhere.

I'm tasting what the Buddhist Scripture says: joy.

The sunflower on my apron twists my body like love.
How are you, my old sun?

As good as in the agrarian age?
From whose eyes wisps this blue smoke?

I don't like the brisk new age, sun.
And this room keeping pace with the world...

A wuthering echo in the morning dew and my sweat—I love
my old kitchen that smelled like a farm
with an empty bottle at dusk. I love

the me that sat still on a small stool.

MD

Pan Wei　潘维

PAN WEI is known for his Southern tone in poetry. He was born in Huzhou, Zhejiang province in 1964, and currently lives in Hangzhou, capital city of Zhejiang, where he teaches. He has published three collections of poetry and has won numerous awards such as the Rou Gang Poetry Prize, Heavenly Question Poetry Prize, and Wen Yiduo Poetry Prize.

SONG OF SHORT REGRET

Make a regret short.
Make it into a centimeter, a millimeter,
a beam of light on the water illuminating only
the back of salmons;
make it into a bird-chirping of early spring
close to the melancholy of hairdressers and widows.

Don't follow the wildfire of Bai Juyi
that brought weeds into history.
Don't tail the Yangtze River that flees day and night.
Don't follow the snails going down south,
slow, slow till death.

Make a regret short.
Cripple the sufferings.
Cool it off in bed.

In the lonely flowering of catkins,
love belongs to other people in this life and the next.

Even if I arrive earlier, it will be always too late,
even if a jade ring is put on her ring finger—
my regret doesn't concern national affairs.

2006

MD

Bai Juyi (772–846 CE), as mentioned in the poem, was a poet in the Tang Dynasty, known for his poem "Song of Long Regret" about the love between Emperor Li and the beautiful Jade-Ring Yang.

Xiao Xiao   潇潇

XIAO XIAO (1964–) started publishing poetry in 1983 and became an editor in the 1990s when she moved to Beijing from Sichuan where she was born and grew up. She edited three volumes of contemporary Chinese poetry and also edited the special anthologies for the Qinghai Lake International Poetry Festival (2007–2015). She has won several poetry awards in China including the Wen Yiduo Poetry Prize (2014).

SPEAKING TO MY SOUL

You must cheer up a million times faster
than you ever possibly can.
Remove the shackles of your long delusions.
Open your eyes from the window of your own prison.
Take a deep breath, and touch your pulse—
listen to the smallest but true heart beat in you.
How many noises are there due to the imagined enemies?
How many infarctions in your flooding blood?
How many necroses from your own darkness?
With one body, one easily shattered mind,
you can't make everything happen.
Write happiness on the back of the envelope of suffering.
Don't let life's tortures kill you.
Live yourself once—for 60 seconds the shortest,
the rest of your life the longest.

2009
MD

Shen Wei 沈苇

SHEN WEI (1965–) was born in Huzhou, Zhejiang Province, but moved to Xinjiang Uyghur Autonomous Region in west China in 1988. He worked as a school teacher, journalist, and now as the editor-in-chief of the regional literary magazine, *The West*. He has published seven books of poetry, the first one winning the first Lu Xun Literature Award in 1998.

CHILDREN OF THE MOON

Each time you return from the moon,
you would whisper to me:
"I've only been to the garden around the corner
for a little while.
A small insect is dying over there . . ."
Phantasy and fantasy.
As if born a pair, you and I can fly
out of this world. But you are light-weight,
much lighter than a cloud, wandering further
while I'm imprisoned even by the air on earth,
planted deep in the field by fate.
Each time you appear with the night dew,
you must've just returned from the moon.
You don't talk about the withering of flowers
or the wretched wind.
It's late fall, there's something in your eyes
that's becoming bluer. Evening chill takes you by the skirt.

You seem far—but even if you are really far away
and the moon and osmanthus trees have died,
I can still smell the scent of your lips.

MD

Zhang Zhihao　张执浩

ZHANG ZHIHAO, born in 1965 in Hubei, central China, graduated from the History Department of Central China Normal University in 1988. He is a staff writer with the Wuhan Writers Union, and executive editor of *Chinese Poetry* quarterly in Wuhan. He won the Chinese Literature Award from the Southern Media Group in 2014, a major award in China.

CARPENTER'S UNIQUE DESIRE

Wood vanishes in the wood shavings.
Trees transform in the wood.
Forests disappear in trees.
Old Zhang's job is to make something
into something else,
turning geometry into an art.
For his whole life he has been making a chair
but he never sits. While standing, he has completed
the life of a craftsman
but never finished a chair.
When I was a boy
I was attracted to the sound he made with his saws.
I asked what he was making.
He said a chair that nobody could sit on.
I asked him when he would finish it. He said tomorrow.
It's tomorrow. I'm a grown up, with calluses on my butt.
But Old Zhang stands in the same place, among the
    shavings.

He takes root there, sprouting here and there.
Tapping and rapping. Some teeth are missing.
Is there such a thing as a chair that nobody can sit on?
I doubt it. But I'd rather believe it.
Some people are always on the move
like a speck of sawdust
looking for its previous life deep in the jungle.

2001

MD, KSK

Shu Cai 树才

SHU CAI (pen name for Chen Shucai) was born in Zhejiang in 1965, and received a PhD in French Literature. He promoted the Third Road in poetry writing. He has translated the poems of Pierre Reverdy, Rene Char and Yves Bonnefoy into Chinese.

FREE SUNDAY

On Sunday I grow wings all over
my body. I read my favorite books
and fly around my room.
I fly. I read the scenery around me.

I come to see this gigantic sea.
On a towering rock
I lay myself down and let more
of nothingness enter my view.

White fleets of ships surge
from the horizon.
They move forward happily
crashing into waves.

A real big bird flies over me.
I'm just sitting, a bird with thoughts
growing from my wings—
it gently lays itself down.

1991
MD, KSK

Yu Xiaozhong　余笑忠

YU XIAOZHONG is one of the finest regional poets in Hubei, central China. Born in a farmer's family in 1965, he graduated from Beijing Broadcasting Institute in 1986 and has worked for Hubei TV since then. He won the 2003 Chinese Poetry Prize awarded jointly by the *Star Poetry Monthly* and *Poetry Monthly*, the third Yangtze River Poetry Prize, and the twelfth edition of the October Literary Prize awarded by *October* magazine.

MURMUR IN THE STORM

Heavy rain scrubs my window over and over again
where I sit, hardly moving.

Far away, thunder seems to urge me
to do something.
Here across the window glass, I see angry storms
like crabs in a hot pot.

At night, lightning blinks to inform me:
in life and death's race
look eye to eye into this immense oblivion.

Night rain falls like inexplicable remorse. In my dream
my late father drags his swollen legs along
while new gigantic stones with old cuts roll down
from high above.

I want to slim down like a crane from the Himalayas,
clear all my internal organs, clean all my bones,
hold my breath—
to climb the snow-capped mountains
over and over.

2015
MD, KSK

Yi Sha　伊沙

YI SHA (1966–) is a major representative of the spoken language school of poetry in China and has published numerous volumes of poetry and several novels. He graduated from Beijing Normal University and has been teaching Chinese literature in Xi-an.

PASSING OVER THE YELLOW RIVER

When the train was passing over the Yellow River
I was in the toilet, pissing.
I know this shouldn't have happened.
I should have been sitting at the window
or standing by the door,
left hand on my hip,
right hand above my eyebrows,
watching like a great man
or at least like a poet,
thinking about what's going on in the river
or some old anecdotes of history.
Everyone was looking out
while I stayed in the toilet
for a long time.
That long moment belonged to me.
I had waited for a whole day and night.
It belonged to me. With my single pee
the Yellow River flowed far away.

1988
MD, KSK

Lei Pingyang 雷平阳

LEI PINGYANG is a very popular poet in China. Born in 1966 in Yunnan, he is a member of the Yunnan Provincial Federation of Literary and Art Circles. He has been promoting his hometown and is well known for a poem about Nanchang River in Yunnan with thirty-seven branches—the whole poem consists of the names of each branch and distance. He has won all the major awards for poetry in China including the Lu Xun Literature Award in 2007.

HAPPY ANTS

In their dreams, they do running drills.
First, over a field. Then, over the
night. For a while they can't see
anything. Some of them are beaten
by the grass, their ribs broken.
In the end, they start to run around the city
in circles. A tiny, little army
that you can neglect. They are being drilled
in their own dreams.

MD

Gu Ma 古马

Gu Ma is the pen name for Cai Qiang, born in 1966 in Gansu, wild wild west China where the Silk Road passed through in the ancient times. His poetry reflects the folk songs in that region. He started publishing poetry in 1986 and won the Fourth Outstanding Literature Award in Gansu province.

A SMALL TOWN WHERE RIVERS RUN BACKWARD

barley for salt
silver for the snow

a horse trotting along for a tea brick
knife for a hand

blood for kinship
brothers for life

stones for a scripture
wind for a deep cry

an eagle for a pair of stirrups
a body for a light weight

earth green again, alas
sheep for the grass

MD

Li Sen 李森

LI SEN (1966–) was born in Yunnan, southwest China, and has lived there all his life, graduating from Yunnan University in 1988 and currently is the Dean of the College of Liberal Arts at Yunnan University. He was a member of the *Them* poetry group with Han Dong and Yu Jian but has been experimenting alone with neoclassical poetry. He has quietly produced several volumes of poetry and essays in remote southwest China. "Tangerine Frontier" has three or four characters a line, a simple form in the *Shi Jing* style (*Book of Songs*, eleventh to sixth century BCE), but also echoes the seven syllable quatrains in the Tang Dynasty, only that it's fragmented as "XXXX / XXX."

TANGERINE FRONTIER

Southeastern sunrise
Tangerine frontier
Yellow is tangerine
Yang is tangerine
Yin is tangerine
Tangerine as if tangerine
Tangerine is the hearth of the greatest house

Western sunset
Tangerine frontier
Sunset with tangerine
Ink-dark expanse with tangerine

Moon at the eaves of the house
Nothing is tangerine

2007
GP

Hu Xian　胡弦

Hu Xian is one of the three most popular poets in China along with Lei Pingyang and Chen Xianfa. Born in Nanjing in 1966, he is the executive editor of *Yangtze River Poetry* in Nanjing. He has been awarded one of the Best Young Poets by *Poetry* monthly in 2009, Wen Yiduo Poetry Prize in 2011, Xu Zhimo Poetry Prize in 2012, Rou Gang Prize in 2014, and the Lu Xun Literature Award in 2018.

ROAD

it's meant to be a road,
a fate anyone can walk.
it's spine and spring, ribs buttoned up, cars
　　heavy on its back.
when all have left, the road remains.
in the darkest nights, it knocks on no one's door.
away and awake,
lonely amidst the traffic,
straighter than class, lower than dirt,
　　wider than tyranny, the road's body
delirious with footsteps.
when the road is told to think, crickets sing.
when forgotten, the road's sky still divides
in two—one way disappears,
the other untaken, bent,
toward time's end.

2010
KY

Chi Lingyun　池凌云

Born in 1966 in a rural area in Zhejiang province, **CHI LINGYUN** started to write poetry in 1985 and emerged as an important poet in that province. She became well known nationally when her second book came out. She works as an editor for the *Wenzhou Evenings* newspaper and has published four collections of poetry.

SONG

now, the surging sea is becoming
a drop of quiet water
not even one song belongs to me
it's dangling over there, small, and even more lovely
in its deep blue capsule
not even one song belongs to me

SUMMER NOTES

Of all the skills, I've learned one only:
to burn.
To burn into ashes, not embers.
I sit in a Zen position, cross-legged, not knowing
how to glow.
I will just disappear, disappear, how else would you
consume me when the flames are dying out,
dying out, dying
out

MD

Yu Nu　余怒

Yu Nu (1966–) is from Anqing City in Anhui Province, a small but ancient city by the Yangtze River in eastern China. He started writing poetry in 1985, and has published two books of poetry. He is known as a poet of post-imagery or deep imagery.

TWO EARTHS

As far as I know there're two earths,
one hanging in the air with ocean water
surging in turbulent waves, the other ice-frozen,
vast and void—inside a mirror.
One has living inhabitants, the other inhabited
by the dead: one reflects light onto the other
as if in a theoretical world, one infers the other
by deduction. One light goes out, the other rises.
That's how they keep a symmetrical balance.
That's how we confirm the creation.
We believe in one of them, ridiculously, and we're
being laughed at by others. We build churches
to commemorate people who have disappeared
before we even get to know them. We're surprised
by each morning that comes on time
and comes again the following day.
We say good morning to each other—hesitantly.
We say it, and yet contradict it in our heart.

2017

MD

Xi Du   西渡

Xi Du (1967–) emerged as one of the campus poets in Beijing in the 1980s. He is originally from Zhejiang province. After graduating from Beijing University in 1989, he has been working as an editor in Beijing till the present time. He has published four books of poetry and three collections of critical reviews. His poetry has been translated into French and published in France as *Songs of Wind and Weeds* (Éditions Fédérop, 2008). He has compiled and edited several important anthologies of poetry, especially the collection of poems by Luo Yihe (1961–1989) in 2011. He won the Liu Li'an Poetry Prize in 1997, the Dong Dangzi Prize in 2014, and the DJS Award for Criticism in 2016.

WATCHING CROWS IN THE SUMMER PALACE

As if all the leaves fly into the sky.
As if all the black-robed monks are murmuring
obscure scriptures. I look up and watch the water
coming to the surface, desolate, across the lake bank.

In this isolated corner, west of the grand
royal garden, as if
dedicated to the bleak winter day,
the crows cry out, circling above.

The whole afternoon I stay by the lakeshore alone.
I clap hands and watch the crows flee through the treetops
casting their gloomy ideas on the clear sky, as if
spreading bills from hell,

demanding reimbursement from humans. They fall
as if ashes flying out of history. I know
they will invade my dreams again at night
requesting words that glorify the darkness.

1994

SMALL BONES IN THE MOONLIGHT

Under the moonlight these tiny bones enter
and come out of my body, like small creatures
on the plains forming little fences.
Penetrated by these tiny fish spears
a fat dolphin falls from the sky
but not a drop of blood dripping and this is my
body, my flesh and blood, my failure in the moonlight.
The tiny bones chase each other,
passing through the saline soil of the moon, like a flock
of helpless orphans
languishing in the water. And these tiny bones flying in a
   V shape
in the imagined wilderness
land on my old desk, like
small pieces of weightless moonlight.

1990
MD, KSK

Chen Xianfa　陈先发

CHEN XIANFA (1967–) holds a high official position as head of the Xinhua News Agency in Anhui province but writes avant-garde poetry. Born in Anhui, he graduated from Fudan University in Shanghai in 1989. He has published three books of poetry, a novel and a collection of essays, and has won numerous awards such as the October Poetry Prize, 1986–2006 Best Ten Poets, Poet of the Year 2008, One of the Best Ten in 1998–2008, and the 2018 Lu Xun Literature Award in the poetry category.

QUESTIONS OF CRANES

Deep in the mountains, I've seen cranes
in the form of pillars. Or even of liquid. Of gas,
or Spring mud curled up at the roots of solemn azaleas,
their wings withdrawn.
I've seen the birds, the fictitious kind,
their pure white color full of rejections, but
growing into a more suitable form on doomsday.

It's a game for dying people to raise cranes,
like a minority religion. Writing poetry
is something else: the "crane"
in this line can be totally replaced. But
never ask what creatures cry for the cranes.
They cry to the east, which is, to the west as well.
They cry for backroom politics, and for street revolutions too

like tonight, in the roaring sound of the fan in my bathroom
I sit for a long time
as if I will never take a step away from here.
I am a worldly man, having never raised a crane or killed one.
I know my suffering is coming to an end with my duties.
I put on a pure white bathrobe, striding to the position
of a bystander, although a former commentator.

2012
MD

Sang Ke 桑克

SANG KE (1967–) is a poet, translator, and poetry critic in Harbin, Heilongjiang Province in northeast China, cofounder of *Poem Life Website* and coeditor of *Poetry Reading Quarterly*. He started writing poetry in 1980 and began to publish in 1985. After graduating from Beijing Normal University in 1989, he has been working for Heilongjiang Daily till the present time. He has published four books of poetry and was awarded the Liu Li-an Poetry Prize in 1997, People's Literature Prize in 2003, and Dong Dangzi Poetry Prize in 2015.

SAME STREET, EVERY MORNING

Cold water runs through the forest
of our time, from the forehead that's so bumpy
to the wasteland of the jaw.
A clear spring of thought
moistens our cracked skin.
He—in an oval mirror of poor quality—
sees an old stranger
looking back at him, making faces
of various expressions.
He keeps quiet, knowing that
the door frame even though deformed
can eavesdrop.

He opens the door and there goes
a long narrow street.
All the pedestrians walk

with footsteps of cotton, aimlessly
toward a bizarre destination.
He sees the dark wheels of a tram
turning like the dazzling needles of morning light
on an ancient record
inside his disordered blood vessels
monitored by an inexplicable wave spectrum—
turning and turning uneventfully
with their innocent eyes looking at the regulated
buildings, pale street lamps, and fresh-looking
children that pass by.

His shoes frayed, he walks
in a sleep-walk-sleep-talk,
carrying weeds on the eve of the weed day.
He walks slowly to the south
of the river, that is to say, a
brilliant inner world, a
point of constraint for both you and me.
He walks slowly.
Wind, with its hand of an octopus,
holds his fingers that look like tree branches.
Oh the warmth from another life—
shows its tired smile
from every drain, every subway entrance,
every deep soul.

1987
MD

Lan Lan 蓝蓝

LAN LAN (pen name of Hu Lanlan) was born in Shandong in 1967, grew up in Henan, and now lives in Beijing. She has published numerous books of poetry, essays, and children's literature and has won a number of poetry awards including the Best Ten Women Poets (2005), and the Yu Long Poetry Prize (2009).

WILD SUNFLOWER

The wild sunflower will fall in the fall,
her head chopped off.
People passing by will suddenly turn
around. It's almost dusk,
her face glowing like golden dust
in the smoky sunset,
distant summer days restored in the skyline.

Passing who? Passing the buckwheat flowers
that go all the way to the horizon?
For whom have I died once again to cover
the sad past? For whom?

The unreal wild sunflower. The unreal
singing
irritates the autumn thorns in my chest.

MD

Li Shaojun 李少君

Li Shaojun advocates for and promotes grassroots poetry, i.e. poetry from the bottom of society. Born in Hunan province in 1967, he graduated from Wuhan University and went to work in Hainan. He has published several volumes of poetry and essays. He was vice-chairman of the Writers Association in Hainan province and currently is associate editor-in-chief of *Poetry Monthly* in Beijing.

GOD COMES TO A SMALL BUS STATION

Three or five cottages,
    one or two lights.
Here I am, as small as an ant, nowhere in the middle
of the grand Hulunbuir Grassland, having to spend a night
    at a nameless station
alone, bearing the cold loneliness but feeling peaceful.

Behind me stands the tiger of a cold winter night.
Behind that is a clear open road.
Behind the road is the Ergun River flowing slowly,
    a shimmering light in the darkness.
Behind that is the endless birch forest,
    the wilderness of wildernesses.
Behind that are quiet stars low in the sky,
    a blue velvet of soft curtain.

And behind that is the vast North where God resides.

2004
MD, KSK

Lin Zi　琳子

LIN ZI was born in 1967 in Henan, central China. She was a middle school teacher, and now a full-time writer. She started publishing her work in 2002, a latecomer but prolific. In 2011, she started to paint and draw. She has made several volumes of drawings to go along with her essays and poems, the most recent one (with poems) won The Most Beautiful Book (2016) in China.

MEMORIAL DAY

It's raining a spring rain this Memorial Day.
The wet petals are washed to the stream
and in this joyous moment I'm that same infant,
barefoot, in your bare arms.

Now I'm standing under a willow tree.
There is a layer of soil between you and me.
You are awake, today, in the soil
like a peach flower.

You are awake in your pink cottons.
You are awake with a full waist.

I won't cry as I know you will incarnate any minute
into a peach tree.
I will not give you a paper horse this time
but a window instead.

MD

Jing Wendong 敬文东

JING WENDONG was born in 1968 in Sichuan. At first, he studied biology and then changed to literature, earning a PhD in 1999. Currently, he teaches at Minzhu University in Beijing. He is the most cutting-edge poetry critic in China today with publication of numerous books of criticism that discuss the most sensitive issues and underrated poets. He was awarded the 2015 Poetry Prize from *Poetry East West*.

A SMALL SKETCH

I always believe in things
that don't exist, such as beginnings, endings...
They steal away my enthusiasm, imagination and
innocence. I appear to be evil
but can be cut to shreds by
even a blade of grass. I'm an alcoholic and a slipshod
half-assed scholar, plus a poet with no license
or title. Every day I dream of landscapes that I didn't yet
crumble. I've worked hard at it for years. Now
I'm walking down a wintery street, stumbling
into the potbelly of middle age.
I'm trying to get back home via a dry twisting road.
I've lost a lot of years
but earned a decent night's sleep.

2003
MD, KSK

Huang Bin　黄斌

Born in 1968 in Redcliff, Hubei Province, central China, **HUANG BIN** studied journalism at Wuhan University and graduated in 1990. He started writing poetry in 1983, won first place in the national poetry competition in 1994, and continues to write poetry while working for *Hubei Daily* as a journalist.

WALKING IN THE WOODS

Walking in the woods in the summer, I see
trees flourishing in a complicated way—
positive, thriving, their interior
grows like human ambitions and swelling desires.
I think of the word 木 *mu*, simple and quiet,
born to be silent, born in the deep fall,
its first appearance stunning. Shocking.
木 *mu* of four seasons slows down to acquire a 木 image.
Look at its shape with branches and a trunk, created
in more than a few days, or a few weeks.
A simple beauty. A holistic miracle. A concrete abstract.
木 lives in the woods, in nature, in the human heart,
immortal in a mortal world.
木 becomes paper, and paper's full of the words 木.
How does 木 in words meet 木 in the woods? How?

MD

Zhu Zhu　朱朱

ZHU ZHU was born in Yangzhou in 1969, and went to college in Shanghai. He lived in Nanjing for many years until he moved to Beijing recently. He is a poet, critic, and curator of art exhibitions and has published numerous volumes of poetry and prose. His honors include the Liu Li'an Poetry Prize, the Chinese Contemporary Art Award for Critics, and the Henry Luce Foundation Chinese Poetry Fellowship at Vermont Studio Center, US.

LITTLE TOWN AS A SAXOPHONE

Men in the rain. With thick, fine hair,
they walk like brown trees, so sparse in the street
that lengthens like a big saxophone.

A ray of light sprawls along the undulating roof.
Threads of rain fall on the children and dogs.
Leaves, and lamps on the wall silently ignite.

I walk into the little town in the highlands.
Along the stairs. Toward the room. On the window is a
    basket of chestnuts.
I walk to the door where a man's lips touch the saxophone.

MD, KSK

Qiu Huadong　邱华栋

QIU HUADONG (1969–) was born and grew up in the Xinjiang Uyghur Autonomous Region, northwest China, and went to Wuhan University in central China. He started writing poetry in middle school and emerged as a writer of urban fiction in the 1990s. A proliferate poet and novelist, Qiu is currently the associate director of the Lu Xun Literary Institute in Beijing.

IN MY POETRY

I want to eat the sunflowers,
the insects and air sacs in the leaves,
the plastic shoes with ideas.
Eat them, eat them all.

I won't give up. I'll eat the nightmares,
the rouge on your face,
the trash in the river.
I'll eat the arc a flying pigeon draws
so it loses track of its nest.

Eat the sailing boat! Eat the tongue itself.
Eat the truth and mist, eat the thinking brain.
Eat the football and the goalkeeper.
Eat the rock and snow on the mountains.
Eat the damned tractor.

Don't forget to eat the street lights, the highways,
the toothpaste and airports,
the gas stations and paratroopers,
sofas, fly swatters, and ancient walls.
Eat all the mirrors!

Eat the entire shore,
the people naked on the beach,
the sandcastle and funny children,
the balloons and the crying women.
Eat them all.

Don't forget to eat yourself.
When I have no tongue, I swallow what I say.

MD

An Qi 安琪

AN QI (1969–) was born Huang Jiangbin in Fujian, and graduated from Zhangzhou Teacher's College in 1988. She currently lives in Tongzhou outside Beijing. She was one of the Third Road Poets, and in recent years a promoter of the Middle Generation (poets born in the mid-1960s)

ME

These new faces, graduates of the ghost news department.
One of them seems to be me. They are taken from drawers,
hung on the tree branches, bodiless, teeth crooked like cookies
cracking, smirking or crying, as if someone was pulling on a string.
These faces of wandering ghosts, with an autocratic quality, dark
but fantastic, as if full of resentment but fully willing.
They provide the world with a background like night,
virtual damp flames, shredded shirts floating around.
"Want to leave the tree? To find the way to the kingdom
of liberty?" You hear someone whisper, holding a flawless torch.
You turn around, bumping into another head.
You—you two—see each other's distorted expression, fear
in the eyes. How long have you been in this tree, dumb,
numb, unconscious? Bones withered or softened.
How long has it been since you graduated from
the ghost news department, drained, strained?
Confession: I was their classmate.

2008
MD, KSK

Jiang Tao　姜涛

JIANG TAO is one of the intellectuals wearing two hats, poet and poet-critic. Born in Tianjin in 1970, he earned a BS in biomedical engineering from Qinghua University in 1994 and a PhD in Chinese literature from Beijing University where he has been teaching since 2002. He also serves as an editor for the *New Poetry Review*, a prominent journal of poetry criticism in China. He won the *Poetry East West Criticism Award* in 2014.

A HOMEBOUND GUY

Somehow I've picked up a not disastrous habit
of walking along a small railway and saying hello in Esperanto
when I meet a yellow dog.
Occasionally a tram passes by and through its windows
I glimpse white-collar beauties
and guess which have been harassed for years.

Well-tended flowers and plants by the roadside,
and convenient public toilets built with local taxes
but on either side two parties stand
sweating and swearing, giving an old partyless bully
a chance to drive the future of this humming city.

I haven't lived here long, not interested in having a share
in the future either—what can I leave behind
with my small casual life style?
So I dream of running into a big fire, a burglar,

a hideous murder; now the police break in
wearing bullet-proof vests and order me to surrender,
but I gasp for air
speaking in a hoarse voice with a foreign accent.
So I'm arrested, humiliated,
kept hooded, made to appear on television,
prosecuted with great fanfare, then quietly withdrawn,
sent on an airplane, extradited to a foreign land of tyranny

where people walk and sleep smugly and triumphantly.
A few exiles have grown gray early—
they are fond of singing "A Drifting Soul"
after a few drinks.

2010

MD, NA, TB

Yu Xiang 宇向

Yu Xiang is one of the most popular poets of her generation in China, known for her minimalist approach to poetry. She was born in Shandong in 1970 and continues to live there today. She has been awarded many prizes including the Rou Gang Poetry Prize in 2002, Top Ten Women Poets in 2004 and the first Yu Long Poetry Prize in 2006.

LOW KEY

a leaf falls—
one leaf falls one night
one leaf falls every night, every season
all leaves fall
down, no sound
as if a man lives alone for a long time, then dies

MD

Ni Zhijuan　倪志娟

Ni Zhijuan is a poet, translator, and a scholar. Born in Hubei in 1970, she currently teaches in Zhejiang. Her first collection of poems came out in 2016, mostly short poems resembling classical poetry in tone and spirit. The book opens with the poem "Swing." Swing is an ancient form of recreational sports, imported to China in the seventh century BCE but it's also very common nowadays, a symbol for free movement. The poem echoes the ancient wisdom, but in contemporary vocabulary. It's almost an eight-line double quatrain, the popular classical form, but she ends at the seventh line making it sound new.

SWING

First the color fades
Then the flower on her lips distills
into a simple smile of abstract lines
She reaches out to hold the quicksand of hours
but it disperses quickly
She holds on to her own hand and takes a swing ride
on the ropes of her own thinking

2005
MD

Xi Wa 西娃

XI WA is one quarter Tibetan from her mother's side. Born in Tibet in 1970, she grew up in Sichuan, and currently lives in Beijing. She published three novels before publishing her first book of poetry in 2016. She was awarded the Li Bai Poetry Prize in 2012 and the Luo Yihe Poetry Prize in 2015.

EATING A TOWER

South China.
We're having a huge
pork tower, shiny red (I prefer
not to remember the name of the dish).
I just can't take my eyes off it. All
the other dishes become its worshipers.
I become its worshiper too. Then I remember
in my birthplace, Tibet,
many believers would gather around a tower
kowtowing and burning incense. I was one of them.
Now I'm one of the many people here.
For years I've cherished the mysterious rituals for temples
and towers
and observed many food taboos.
But now look at this red, shiny tower
of pork—
this human appetite: people eat everything
eatable
or not eatable.

Now they are raising it, sharing the pork
in the shape of a tower, red,
shiny.
All sound silenced, I only see
in the dusty smoke my faith
is filling the stomachs of
another mankind—
they're swallowing it
into their bodies
fearlessly.

2012
MD, KSK

Jiang Hao　蒋浩

JIANG HAO (1971–) is a poet, essayist, editor, and book designer. Born in Chongqing, he has wandered around the country and finally settled in Hainan (South Sea Island). He has published one collection of essays and four poetry collections, winning first place in the Beijing Arts International Poetry Awards in 2014. He wrote a sequence of poems from 2006 to 2014 while wandering around, all titled "Poem of Wandering Immortals" which was popular in ancient times in terms of subject matter and style. The Chinese *xian* has multiple meanings: fairies, wonderland, and immortals. Li Bai (701–762) wandered around in the wonderland to avoid and satirize the reality of his time (Tang Dynasty). So does Jiang Hao today. The form Jiang Hao has created is fourteen lines in the Upper part and fourteen lines again in the Lower part. A division of Upper and Lower used to be popular in the Song Dynasty. Observation first, then philosophical thinking and free association. Jiang Hao has made most of his upper parts metaphysical, and most of his lower parts physical (upper as in the brain and lower as in the lower body) with a few exceptions. The fourteen lines are not sonnets but in his self-made structure of 5–5–4. In other words, he is making his turning point of the Song dynasty standard of "opening, responding, turning, and closing" at a different point, thus achieving a freshness. The abundant use of archaic vocabulary mixed with contemporary jargon and strange imagination makes his poems almost new neoclassical.

POEM OF WANDERING IMMORTALS

Upper

He lies down with clothes on, accidentally catching thorns
and blossoms, young branches hanging down from Leo
as if injecting gravity into the body of a reed. A cactus
floating in soap bubbles gets rid of its needles unconsciously
while the bath towel finds no worries in its four horns,
provoking four seasons of reincarnations.

It's late spring, or autumn. A bamboo bird, incidentally,
pecks at the nuclear power from the enduring ripples
of the hydropower plant: one circle a year, planting lotuses
like practicing a cyclical theory. The valley's mouth resembles
a white undergarment on a branch, the black iron gate outputs
burning waves of catastrophes.

You either shower your top like winning a top lottery
or tailor to your body's six corners and win a Mark Six.
A lightning rod hides in a pub. A sewing machine
sews pavilions, long and short, until a climbing ivy
ambushes politics; a fire cloud blocks the way removing
all moralities and authorities.

Lower

Oh a passage? A kitchen with floating breasts. Clouds.
Dark aprons like battling cities. Stars fall into an oil pan
forging iron. Soy sauce and vinegar stagger like
yin and *yang*. On the plate a bridge stands up.
Beautiful? Like a pier? A lawn mower licks the sewer,
a fence built in the nowhere of its bee slim waist.

You love food, love its lusty colors, its ingredients as integrities.
On the cherry cheerful terrace a straw draws water
from a withered tree, inviting the red thread girl to light up
the ghost lamp when a Buddhist jumps over the wall.
Gingers, leeks and garlic look like him and you and me, a floor of
chicken feathers. Bowls and dishes and plates, spouses of
    replications.

Ah the recipes possess a gluttonous order like demons.
The picture books look embarrassingly ancient
and stylish. All those wrinkled skins have retained
stormy rains. In the telescope is an upside down mirage
where a hand sketching is stirring ink in the coffee.
Is this poetry?

2010

MD

Xuanyuan Shike   轩辕轼轲

Xuanyuan Shike is a member of the Lower Body Poetry group. He was born in Shandong in 1971 and grew up there. He launched a magazine with his friends in 1999 named *Middle* but joined the Lower Body movement in 2000. He has published three books of poetry and won the poetry prize from the *Peoples' Literature* magazine in 2012.

A UNIVERSE THAT COMES LATE

There is another universe
outside ours, half a beat slower
where babies are born late
and trees grow slowly
No high-speed trains. No freeways
To visit a neighbor, you need to carry some food
Marathon? Might as well be walking
Walking? Might as well be pacing around
The clock's second hand moves like the sun
taking a long time to move a single step

There're never queues before windows
Things are done slowly, might as well not be done at all
so that no one will need a document
You can easily go abroad but never reach a border in your life
You can easily go astray but can never get out of your family circle
There is no smog in the sky
Smoke gets exhausted before climbing out of the chimney
People speak slowly

Their brains don't make sharp turns
If you see a friend and say hello
you can go to a slow food restaurant on the roadside
When you finish eating and get outside
you will then hear his response

Of course the slowest person is the Prime Minister
His inaugural speech is not drafted
until his term is almost over
If he is going out to meet the public
he will have to hold his own loud speaker and yell for three days
until he can get a
slower bodyguard

MD, KSK

Lü Yue　吕约

Lü Yue wears two hats: spoken language poet and feminist poet. She was born in 1972 in Hubei and graduated from East China Normal University in Shanghai in 1993 with a major in Chinese literature. She worked for a news media organization for over ten years and currently works for the October Literary Institute in Beijing.

POETRY DOESN'T KNOW THAT IT'S DEAD

Poetry doesn't know that it's dead.
A state funeral is taking place on a 1000-hole golf course,
its eyelids are sprinkled with petals, and on the petals a few
　teardrops,
one from Greek, one from Latin
and the rest from crocodiles.
An epitaph is written in Chinese oracle script.
All that have two legs have witnessed its death, it died finally
shrouded in black and gold,
its mouth faintly grinning.

Grasshoppers are alive, so are lizards and butterflies.
All that crawl or fly are alive.
Dinosaurs are walking to the zoo with children for a spring outing,
their small bellies bulging with fresh milk.
The Pope is alive, on his way to Africa by air.
Africa is alive.
Robots of the ninth generation will be alive too.
Poetry is dead, but doesn't know it yet.

Still dreaming of parachuting in heaven with all the living,
small or pregnant.
Still dreaming of shooting off rockets.
Of running marathons in Third World streets
with a bulletproof vest.

In the funeral a child sees poetry still rolling its eyes
under its lids.
It has donated its corneas—
it will never see its own death

2007
MD, NA

Han Bo 韩博

HAN BO (1973–) is a poet, playwright, and visual artist. Born in Harbin, Heilongjiang province, he went to college in Shanghai where he currently lives. He earned an MA in Journalism from Fudan University in Shanghai and attended the International Writers Workshop in Iowa in 2009. He was awarded the Liu Li'an Poetry Prize (1998) and the *Poetry East West* Poetry Prize (2012).

MORNING

Sun ripens on the teeth
of corn as Grandma
sets table for breakfast.
Strawberries in clean water
with melons and golden berries.
Salad of green string beans
wakes me up, the whole summer spreading ahead.
Grandma talks about the poppies on the balcony,
in an aged pot with black patterns.
My mother's mother has a bright mind, a full house
of children and grandchildren.
She tastes the same fruit of the same flowers everyday,
her body transformed into a mountain forest
or a witch
obsessed with TV news. Yesterday
I was almost digested by an iron bird in its stomach,
even my dream didn't escape.
This morning, there's a cloud market on my pillow,

morning glories singing for the iron bird in a sunken sky.
Crickets chirp in a northern accent
calling for the shrinking shadow of the sun.
We gather in the square hall,
only Grandpa is missing. The smell of vegetation
passes through the hall
and our dining table. Old stories ring a bell.
Five years ago, fifty years ago . . . Grandma speaks in a
    flashback,
naïve, and lovely,
Grandpa carrying a pistol
knowing who's singing to cheer him up.

MD

Leng Shuang 冷霜

LENG SHUANG (1973–), poet and critic, was born in Xinjiang Uyghur Autonomous Region. He went to Beijing University for a BA and PhD in Chinese literature and currently teaches at Minzhu University in Beijing. He is also an editor for the *New Poetry Review* in Beijing.

REREADING MANDELSTAM

Heavy trucks rumble far off
like combers washing ashore.
Only me on the lake's first ice
trembling with the earth.
How fine it is, this thin light
still carrying the warmth of distant years
and splashing into my eyes—in the cold
air I see the pointed face of a star!

2003
TB, MD

Quan Zi 泉子

Quan Zi is the chief editor of *Poetry Construction Quarterly*, a new dynamic magazine that has quickly earned a reputation in China. His daytime job is at Hangzhou airport. He meditates in his poetry and travels to ancient China, but mostly questions the morality of current society. He was born in 1973 in Zhejiang and has published four books of poems and two books of essays.

ANCIENT SUSPICION

When you get out of the car, a cup of wine
will greet you. Dip your ring finger in.
Fillip up to worship the heavens.
Fillip down to worship the earth.
Touch your forehead to worship your ancestors.
But you know the origin of this ritual?
It's from the legend of Genghis Khan's father.
Older than the legend was an ancient grassland custom.
All horsemen, when passing by a herdsman's banquet,
known or unknown, would join in for a drink.
They would greet the host and share their joy.
Genghis Khan's father died this way.
He died from an enemy's poisoned wine.
Folks have since invented a new ceremony.
They wear a silver ring on their ring finger.
They worship the heavens, the earth, their ancestors.
They observe the ring's changing colors—
to avoid what happened to Khan's father.

The tourist guide tells us about this grassland etiquette
on our journey to the Mongolia Plateau.
I'm overtaken suddenly by a tremendous sadness—how
blind trust, so beautiful and ancient, has degenerated to
such distrust.

2012
MD, KSK

Chen Jun　陈均

CHEN JUN specializes in Kun Opera, a form of theatre in the six-tenteen to eighteenth centuries in central China. He was born in Hubei, central China, in 1974, went to Beijing University for his PhD in literature, and currently teaches art history there, with publications of one novel, two collections of poetry and two collections of essays.

SUMMER

The swinger the swirler the swirled: stop grieving.
I drink all night but with a diminishing appetite.
The scene outside is obscene from a humble window.
My sentiment spreads, my famine a flagpole.
Birds sing next year's songs, or antique rescues.
I write but where shall I send it?
Let go—I shall go tie the flowers the leaves the whole orchard.
The outskirts are curved, shadows of countrywoman donors . . .
You bring me a cup of fresh tea that I love
I return you two kapok leaves—like hand waves.

2009

IN THE KITCHEN

Early in the morning, a dough rises
from the bowl, swirling. He stretches his
bean paste fists, his mouth
dripping a black cocoa stream . . .
Hey, I say, have you just smuggled
nine knife mountains and nine oil pans from hell?
Deep-fried ghosts are the sweetest the crispiest the most intelligent
even in burnt rims, and taste even better with soy bean drinks.
He droops his sad expressions
like Oedipus with a cane. Collapsed
in the steamer, he squeaks out a sweet smell
of duck soup from his soul—quack, quack.

2009
MD

Hu Xudong 胡续冬

HU XUDONG (1974–) is a poet and Spanish/Portuguese translator. Born in Sichuan, he attended college and graduate school at Beijing University where he is currently teaching Portuguese literature. He has published six books of poetry and a few collections of essays. He was a visiting professor at the University of Brasilia (Brazil) (2003–2005), a participant in the International Writing Program at the University of Iowa (2008), and visiting professor at the National Central University of Taiwan (2010).

MAMA ANA PAULA ALSO WRITES POETRY

A corn husk pipe in mouth, she throws a thick poetry book
at me, "Read your Mama's poems."
This is true, my student
José's mother,
two Brazils on her chest, a South America on her bucks,
a stomach full of beer, surging like the Atlantic,
this Mama Ana Paula
writes poetry. The first day I met her, she lifted me
up like an eagle
catching a small chicken, I wasn't informed She Writes Poetry.
She spat her wet words at me, and rubbed
my face
with her big palm tree fingers. When she licked my
panicked ears
with marijuana tongue, I didn't know She Writes Poetry.
Everyone including her son José and daughter-in-law Gisele said

she was an old Flower Silly, but no one
told me She Writes Poetry.
"Put my teacher down, my dear old Flower Silly." José said.
She dropped me, but went on
vomiting "dick" "dick", and catching "dick"
in the air with her lips. I looked at her
back, strong like a hairy bear that kills
a bull even when she's drunk, and I understood:
She Writes Poetry.
But today, when I followed José into the house, and caught a glimpse
of her lying by the pool
with four limbs stretched out, smoking, I didn't think She Writes
    Poetry
I ran into a ponytail
like Bob Marley, a muscle guy, in the living room, Gisele told me
that's her mother-in-law's guy from last night, I didn't think, even if
you shoot at my little torso, that Mama Ana Paula
writes poetry. But Mama Ana Paula
Mama Anna Writes Poetry Paula
writes poetry
which burps and farts. I leafed it through page after page
Mama Ana Paula's poetry book. Yes, Mama Ana Paula writes poetry
indeed. She doesn't write fat poetry, liquor poetry,
marijuana poetry, dick poetry, or muscle poetry of muscle guys.
In a poem called "Three Seconds of Silence in Poetry"
she wrote: "Silence in a poem—give me a minute and in it
I can spin the nine yards of sky."

2004, *Brasília*
MD, KF

Qin Xiaoyu　秦晓宇

QIN XIAOYU (1974–), poet, essayist, and now filmmaker. He was born in Inner Mongolia and currently lives in Beijing. He has published a collection of essays and a collection of poetry, coedited an anthology of Contemporary Chinese Poetry with Yang Lian and edited an anthology of migrant workers' poetry alone.

THE ROCK ARTIST

I carve my prey into the rocks,
so the animals, now fur coats, are conquered by me again.

The lines of dead trees, jagged as if broken at intervals.
Fear has beautiful forms.

I paint the antlers into dense woods,
so the deer from rock cliffs roam between their foothills.

I paint the slow: the sun descending between the peaks.
I let the evening light find its color.

And the fast are the slender lines of riders and horses
which seem to be able to shorten the roads.

I carve-paint what surprises me, and my wide-eyed surprise too.
I love to paint what I love to do most: like a gecko on a wall.

I paint masks to help green things grow
and make the world simple and brief.

2013
NA, MD

Mu Cao　墓草

MU CAO (1974–) is one of the very few gay writers in contemporary China. He was born Su Xianghui in rural Henan, and moved to Beijing to pursue a literary career. He has published a novel, a collection of short stories, and three book of poetry. He fights for gay rights through his writing.

FAREWELL

He is a man of flowers
using a language of fruit
even though miserable,
and he smells like mint ice cream.
He has no traces on his face
to betray who he is
but one drink brings him
to me.

He can't drink any more he says.
He has diabetes he says,
getting dialysis each day he says.
I hug him, the man of flowers,
and feel the groan deep in his crotch.

2014
MD

Shen Haobo 沈浩波

SHEN HAOBO (1976–) is a well-known entrepreneur poet, born in Jiangsu province, and graduated from Beijing Normal University. He wrote a critical essay as a college student that started a huge debate in 1999, known as the Panfeng debate, between spoken language poets and the intellectual writing group. He has been a major advocate and representative poet of the Lower Body Poetry since 2000 even though his recent writing seems to have shifted from body to mind. He is the founder of X-iron, an independent publishing house in Beijing.

TOKYO

In Tokyo there are as many
crows
as gravestones
but crows are lucky
if the comparison isn't.
So many crows and naked legs
of women. The streets are full
of fallen cherry blossoms—
on the pale petals
are white legs
and black
shoes.

CHESSBOARD

I'm flying back to Beijing
and looking out—
I see a thin layer of whiteness
over the city. Snow.
A chessboard.
But who is playing chess
with me? Nobody, only me
and the bloody setting sun—
watching each other
across the snowboard.

2016
MD

Yu Xiuhua　余秀华

Yu Xiuhua (1976–) was born with cerebral palsy in the rural area of Hubei Province in central China. She started writing poetry in 2009 and became well known in 2014 with her online poem "Crossing Half of China to Sleep with You". Her debut book came out in early 2015 with 15,000 copies sold in one day. She was awarded the annual national Poetry Prize in 2015 and the Haizi Poetry Prize in 2016 in China, and was selected by the *New York Times* in 2017 as one of the eleven most courageous women around the world.

CROSSING HALF OF CHINA TO SLEEP WITH YOU

To sleep with you or to be slept, what's the difference if there's any?
Two bodies collide—the force, the flower pushed open by the force,
the virtual spring in the flowering—nothing more than this
and this we mistake as life restarting. In half of China
things are happening: volcanoes
erupting, rivers running dry,
political prisoners and displaced workers abandoned,
elk deer and red-crowned cranes shot.
I cross the hail of bullets to sleep with you.
I press many nights into one morning to sleep with you.
I run across many of me and many of me run into one to sleep with you.
Yet I can be misled by butterflies of course
and mistake praise as spring,
a village like Hengdian as home. But all these,
all of these are absolutely indispensable
reasons that I sleep with you.

ON THE THRESHING FLOOR, I CHASE CHICKENS AWAY

And I see sparrows fly over. They look around
as if it's inappropriate to stop for just any grain of rice.
They have clear eyes, with light from inside.
Starlings also fly over, in flocks, bewildered.
They flutter and make a sound that seems to flash.
When they're gone, the sky gets lower, in dark blue.
In this village deep in the central plain
the sky is always low, forcing us to look at its blue,
the way our ancestors make us look inside ourselves,
narrow and empty, so we look out again
at the full September—
we're comforted by its insignificance but hurt by its smallness.
Living our life this way, we feel secure.
So much rice. Where does it come from?
So much gold color. Where does it come from?
Year after year I've been blessed, and then deserted.
When happiness and sadness come in the same color code, I'm happy
to be forgotten. But who am I separated from?
I don't know. I stay close to my own hours.

MD

Zhang Er 张尔

Born in Anhui Province in 1976, **ZHANG ER** currently lives in Shenzhen publishing an independent poetry journal and curating poetry readings. He won the *Poetry East West* Poetry Prize in the category of Editing/Curating in 2016.

REALITY

One day, or forever—my camera lenses grow pinholes
overlooking the world as if in a boundless darkroom.
By the shore, sturgeon expose their scales
with tightened bodies. Their bones fall apart onto a plate,
separate, and then blare in one tune.
Financial scarlet fever curves like silk balls, flirting.
A minor official waves a proletarian weight, tearfully,
making sentences underground, lighting a fire.
After snow, poetry is a coal mine of words sliding into a dump.
Your palms sweat, cooling down the residual social warmth.

2013
MD, KSK

Jiang Li　江离

JIANG LI (1978–), pen name of Lü Qunfeng, was born in Zhejiang in eastern China. He earned an MA in philosophy from Zhejiang University and became the executive editor of *Poetry Jiang Nan* (Southern River) and a founding editor of *Poetry Construction* in 2011.

GEOMETRY

— for Cai Tianxin

After the snow storm, I move to the mountaintop
and stroll among the blue and white stars
every evening. They move slowly
like caravans in the desert, a decrepit orange color
that we've never seen in the woods.
A neighbor grown distant is gone.
I worry, and even my worry seems superfluous.
In my notebook, I faithfully record
births, deaths,
and the delicate balance in between.
There seems to be a structure: each of them exists
in another. Solitude
must become part of a greater friendship.
And for immortality, time must be redivided.
In my room, the tables and chairs in chaos
form another expression of clarity.

2002

MD, NA

Li Hongwei　李宏伟

LI HONGWEI (1978–) was born in Sichuan and graduated from the Renmin University in Beijing with an MA in philosophy. He currently lives in Beijing working as a literary editor. He has published a book of poems, a novel, and a collection of short stories. He won the Xu Zhimo poetry award in 2014.

DREAMING OF A TIGER'S CORPSE

Those who dream of tigers on a rainy day
possess an ancient forest inside their bodies
where there are hundreds of green, lush woods and calm birds.
Sunrays are packed, unable to find a way to flow out.
Even if they poke through the leaves and pour to the ground
there would be only colorful tapestry stitches.

The father of the public beasts rises.
He walks at ease, eyes far-reaching.
He doesn't carry weapons, just his flashing teeth.
With his howling, he patrols the vast dream
and with a real tail, left and right,
mopping the fern grass and earth, sweeping the wind.
He leaps up to the crouching boulder, and
with one big bite eats up the rain and the dreamers.

It's on a raining day like this,
I dream of a tiger's corpse.
Ragged, it's halfway immersed in a paddy field,

two hind legs completely empty.
Luckily, his mouth and wiring are intact.
With electricity, it can smile a tiger smile
and sing soaking-wet songs.

MD, KSK

Ma Yan　马雁

MA YAN (1979–2010), poet and essayist, was a Muslim from Chengdu. She graduated from Beijing University. She died in Shanghai due to illness. Her collections of poems and essays were published posthumously by her friends.

WEDDING

It's a rainy night and we walk down the street,
eating loquat fruit. We are in love every spring
night. There is nothing to see around us,
yet my face isn't pale at all. You tell me
life is dull and it sends me a text message
every morning about the weather—
the weather for us to be in love—every day is good
for loving each other. Every day, I should
hold an umbrella for you, leaning on your shoulder.
There are also thick quilts, good for us
to lie inside, touching each other, like touching
one's own familiar chest, and from there
the gift of constant warmth gushes out.
Without this timely rain to rescue the situation,
my dear, I would panic to death. Only in death,
my dear, can you order me to live. So I have no other
choice but to die, with big ice cubes in my mouth.

2004
MD, KSK

Zheng Xiaoqiong 郑小琼

ZHENG XIAOQIONG is a well-known migrant worker poet in China. Born in rural Sichuan in 1980, she moved to Dongwan City in southern Guangdong Province as a migrant worker in 2001 and began to write poetry about her factory life. She won the Liqun Literature Award from *Peoples' Literature* in 2007 and became known nationwide and in recent years internationally.

INDUSTRIAL ZONE

The white light is on, the building is lit, the machine is on,
my fatigue is lit, the blueprint is lit . . .
It's Sunday night, the night of August 15th,
the moonlight is on, a full hollow of emptiness, the lychee tree is lit,
a breeze blows the clear emptiness in its body while silence keeps
its year-round quietness, only insects sing in the bushes.
All the lights are on, the city is lit, so many dialects in the industrial
zone, so many humble people weak and homesick.
The industrial city. Sunday night.
The moonlight is on, the machine is lit, the blueprint is lit,
my face is lit—the rising moon lights up my falling heart.

Many lights are on, many people are passing by.
The lights in the industrial zone, my past my present the machine
the silent moonlight the silent lights the small me so small,
a piece of metal, a tool, a lamp—I warm up the industrial city
with my frail body. The bustling the noise the liveliness,

my tears my joy my pain,
my brilliant humble thoughts. My soul is lit
by the moonlight. It collects my thoughts and takes them to a far away
place. They diminish and disappear in the light, unnoticed.

2011

MD

Xiao Shui　肖水

XIAO SHUI is a representative poet of the post-80 generation. Born in 1980 in Hunan, he went to Fudan University in Shanghai, and currently teaches there. He founded the Fudan Poetry Festival and the Fudan Poetry Library. He is promoting the annual Fudan poetry competitions for college students nationwide.

FOOD IS RUNNING OUT

Food is running out
I have to tell you
what we are facing
Corn, wheat, potatoes
and rice, all these we live on
but never produce are gone. Hunger comes
like the fireworks you've never seen
Hunger is the food tomorrow gives us today
But before it's completely dark
and the sun not set, the mountains are already black
Don't say this is the last banquet
that you need to be dressed up
Don't say the knives and forks and plates
are just being manufactured
Before the moon has come out, we
have an opportunity to be opportunists
We can step into the autumn rice fields
in the South, or the storms
There will always be a way to the distant warehouse

There will always be robbers and a furious judge
There will always be coffins and verses of praise
There will always be rice when we wake up from sleep
in the properties stolen by the mouse
in the lullabies the peasants are no longer singing
in the hands of the beggars, between their fingers
The rice will fly up with the ghosts of our ancestors, and
land in a paddy field of moist words
All night, in the darkness
surrounded by fatigue, I wait
for one word after another to sprout
Before they open up, flowering, growing into
great lines on Du Fu's mustaches,
or clear moonlight in Li Bai's glass—
I pick them up and quickly stuff them into my mouth
Food is running out
I stretch out my hands and turn to Time
I know I'm more hungry than the rice granary
and more fatigued—will you cry for me

2003
MD

Yuan Yongping 袁永苹

YUAN YONGPING (1983–) stands out among the young poets in China with fresh language and imageries in her poetry. She was born and lived in Harbin, northeast China. She was a journalist there before moving to Beijing a few years ago and currently she works as a poetry editor for a growing publisher in Beijing. She has published poems in many journals and was awarded the DJS First Poetry Book in 2012 for her book titled *Private Life*.

EVENING PRAYER

Today I see you pray in your father's style.
You curl up when we play
peekaboo in bed. I pull up your little jacket and see your
little pearl-ribs, bent, your spine extending
to a pale arrangement toward your little smile.
Soon you start to cry and that's our evening ritual.
The moon is high, not yet in the clouds,
spilling a golden ray on the blue tops of factory shops,
sparkling. Ten thousand things quiet down
like peaceful ocean waves
waiting, with us,
for the high tide to sail into sleep.

MD

Li Heng　黎衡

LI HENG is one of the most gifted young poets in China today. Born in 1986 in Shiyan, Hubei, he graduated from Wuhan University and currently works as a journalist in Guangzhou, southern China. His poems have been widely published and anthologized, winning him the Liu Li-an Poetry Prize, the Weiming Poetry Prize, the China Times Literary Award, and the DJS-*Poetry East West* Award.

BUS IN A STORM

To get away from the heavy rain
on the emptied platform,
I run and squeeze into
a bus
that's going somewhere I have no idea of.
It speeds up, making a turn
across the bridge,
eager to prove that it's got nothing to do
with the rain.
But the shadow of the stormy rain
has turned into a blind man
playing this underwater bus-piano,
striking the passengers—black and white keys
of various shapes,
and they (that is, we) will wake up
out of tune and tone
when the bus stops.

2014
MD, KSK

Jike Bu 吉克·布

JIKE BU (1986–), birth name Jike Ayibujin, is of Yi nationality. She was born and grew up in Xichang, Yi autonomous region of Sichuan province, and went to college in Chengdu and later to graduate school in Chongqing, being the first Yi woman specializing in art. Currently she teaches art at the Xichang Normal College, the only college in the Big Cold Mountain region. She started publishing poems while in college and became known as one of the best Yi poets of the younger generation. Jike Bu speaks Yi as her mother tongue but writes poetry in Han Chinese.

CALL HER SUOMA

Call her Suoma
in the name of love we share
in the last, this and next life.
Love her—love her breathtaking color
                    from blooming,
the traces she left
in the wind the rain the scorching sun.
Nothing distains her beauty: she is pure
like ice jade
but she is not just pretty and frail.
Her sonorous voice comes from the air,
the revolving stream, the soil.
Love her.
And embrace her barren body
like heaven and earth

and everything that grows on earth
with natural birth and death
in the world even though the world
doesn't care where the wind blows,
where you're from what you are or where you're going.
She has her own garden, her old dream
and her clearly sounding name—
Call her Suoma out loud
like calling yourself.

MD

Suoma, *as mentioned in the title, means* azalea flower *in the Yi language. It's also the most common name for women in the Yi region in China.*

Kawa Niangji ལ་གས་ཀྱི་ཉེན་ཕྱིས།

KAWA NIANGJI 卡瓦娘吉 (1989–2015) is the pen name for Niangjiben ལ་གས་ཀྱི་ཉེན་ཕྱིས།, a Tibetan poet and environmental activist from Qinghai province. He published a book of fairy tales in the Tibetan language, titled *Flying Moths*, in 2014, and published poems and prose in his blog in Chinese. He drowned in Qinghai Lake on June 26, 2015, at age twenty-six, while trying to dismantle an illegal fishing net for Huang fish—they are a key element in keeping the ecological balance in the Qinghai Tibetan region.

THE FINAL JUDGMENT

I'm waiting for doomsday,
for things to become nothing.
When a big bang bangs in outer space
we'll all be back to the beginning, everything quiet.

At the very end of time, I'll start
all over again, bringing with me food,
hope, and light, and bringing with me
a healthy body and a good spirit.

I need a harbor
to settle my wandering soul.
I need a bed, five feet three inches long,
a quilt, a woman, a family.

All these and everything else are emptiness.
Cry out! So I cry all night
and my tears become an ocean, never dry.
But I don't remember why I'm in such pain.

2015
MD, KSK

Xu Lizhi 许立志

Xu Lizhi (1990–2014) was a migrant worker in Shen Zhen, born in Jieyang, Guangdong. He published poems while working in factories from 2010–2014. He left two hundred poems to his young legacy.

I SWALLOW AN IRON MOON

I'm swallowing an iron moon,
a screw they call it.
I'm swallowing industrial wastewater, unemployment, orders.
People die young, who are shorter than the machines.
I'm swallowing migration, displacement,
skywalks and rusty life.
I can't swallow any more. All that I've swallowed rush out
of my throat
spreading like a shameful poem
on my fatherland.

2013
MD

Qin Sanshu　秦三澍

Born in Jiangsu province in 1991, **QIN SANSHU** is currently a graduate student of comparative literature in Shanghai and Paris, and head of a student poetry club at Fudan University. He won the DJS-*Poetry East West* Poetry Prize (in the Young Poet category) in 2015. He translates poetry from French and English and writes critical reviews for poetry magazines.

LATE SUPPER

Come through the narrow door where I speak
of sins.

For three months my memory has lingered
on this oiled table, now incinerated.
You've put on fake flames to show how you love me

and you've broiled me. I feel hard and hot.
The half-cooked soup rejects my tongue,
the guilty organ, and forgives

the me that shrinks inside my atrophic body, a kernel
in a rain forest. The gathering storm
touches my tears, then the thunder. I do not ask for mercy—

Vegetable leaves, the almighty, come to cover me.

But stop. My one-sided body is unable
to finish the net-shaped supper,
torn between grief and loving. My face is
sliding into the water, eaten by the fish, so thin.

Stop when you reach the pond. The rain
seems to be falling upside down to bring back the dead lotus.

MD

Su Xiaoyan　苏笑嫣

SU XIAOYAN (1992–) is ethnically Mongolian, a young poet born in Liaoning and currently lives in Beijing. Her Mongolian name is Mu Xiya 慕玺雅. She moved to Beijing with her parents during her middle school years and started to publish poems while a teenager. She wrote a novel based on her experience as a drifter in the capital city, being forced to return to her hometown, lost in between. She was finally admitted to Beijing Industrial Institute and now works as a designer in Beijing. She has published two novels, two collections of essays and one collection of poems.

TWO BAMBOO BASKETS

Like two old men, the two bamboo baskets sit
side by side on a wooden bench by the door
looking quietly at the cornfield—
a flying bird passes by, singing.
They gaze into their favorite slow breeze in the afternoon,
tranquility dispersed in the air, the yellowed years.

The two aged bamboo baskets have year after year
loaded so many things: banana pears,
banana apples, and pearl-like peanuts.
Now they are empty, the bamboo sticks stunned,
their bodies wrapped with hemp ropes,
fatigued and lifeless.

In the past they fell deeply in love with the fall
but now they fall in the shadow of the season
that has changed instantly, from warm to desolate,
the memories framed on the trees
as they harvest year after year and have harvested
an entire life, now blown

away by a gust of wind.
A tree full of fruit, and two bamboo baskets:
they don't know how they can be loaded again.
For the first time they face the harvest
at a loss, but calmly.

MD

From butterflies to living words
Rereading Hu Shi

IT'S HARD TO BELIEVE that what we call avant-garde poetry today started a hundred years ago. But a hundred years is a short period of time when we look at the three thousand years' tradition of what's called classical poetry that preceded the modern era. In 1915–1916, a group of Chinese students in the United States were engaged in a heated debate about whether or not everyday plain speech (vernacular language) should be used in poetry writing and whether the "old shoes" of classical forms still fit. Hu Shi 胡适 (1891–1962), a philosophy student at Columbia University during those years, started writing free verse, allegedly influenced by *Poetry*, which was started by Harriet Monroe in Chicago in 1912. He published "A preliminary proposal for literary reform" in the prominent journal *New Youth* (La Jeunesse) in China in January 1917, followed by eight poems in the February issue. He returned to China in July 1917 to promote a literary revolution and became one of the most influential figures in the May Fourth New Cultural Movement of 1919, which demanded democracy and freedom. In October 1919, he published an essay titled "On New Poetry." In 1920, the first anthology of New Poetry was published, followed by Hu Shi's own collection of New Poetry, *Book of Experiments*. A hundred years later we are still writing New Poetry and experimenting with it, for better or worse.

Today, all schools of poets in China, left and right, governmental or independent, unanimously consider 1917 as the beginning of the current avant-garde poetry. And Hu Shi is acknowledged as the first poet of New Poetry, and his first poem in the 1917 publication, "Butterflies," as the first New Poem in China. But very few people like this Butterfly poem; and nobody takes him as a great poet because most of the poems in his first book resemble the "Butterflies." I'm not motivated to translate it either but will just give a basic idea here:

> Two yellow butterflies take off as a pair.
> One suddenly returns from the sky
> leaving the other one alone in despair
> with no more desire to further fly.

What Hu Shi considered revolutionary in this poem was a break away from the tradition of "one poem one rhyme" by alternating abab. But it sounds like a nursery rhyme today. So I took the accepted view of regarding him as a poor poet in the preface of *New Cathay: Contemporary Chinese Poetry* (Tupelo Press, 2013). But three months after the anthology was published, I saw Hu Shi's *Student Diaries* (Chinese edition, Taipei: Shanghai Bookstore Press, 1937) and was surprised to find his other poems completely different, especially a long one written on July 22, 1916, a month before he wrote the butterfly poem. I would now regard this as his first true New Poem, and this is what his New Poetry was meant to be.

Reply to Old Mei—A Poem in Plain Speech
(答梅觐庄—白话诗)

Days are getting cool, people less busy,
Old Mei starts a fight and accuses Hu Shi
of being too ridiculous in saying
that "Living literature is what China needs,"

that "Writing must be in the way people talk!"
Who says there are living words and dead words?
Isn't the vernacular too vulgar?

...

Old Mei complains, while Hu Shi laughs out loud.
Cool down man, how can you talk so loud
with such an outdated tone?
Words may not be old or new, but definitely dead
or alive.

...

A living text is what you know and can talk about.
A dead text is what you have to translate.
Texts of three thousand years, up and down, living or dead,
who knows how many have been hijacked.

...

I dare not argue, nor dare ignore.
I have to speak out. Not speaking out is not a way out.
Don't you dare laugh
at a poem in plain speech. It beats
a hundred books of the Southern Society texts.

This was a declaration of free verse in vernacular Chinese. South Society (1909–1923) mentioned at the end of the poem was a poetry organization that Mei Jinzhuang (Old Mei) belonged to at that time, where most of the poets were writing in old, bookish Chinese.

While most of Hu Shi's published poems are short and simple, "Reply to Old Mei" has 106 lines divided into five parts, and it is not only long but much more interesting with citations of major literary works in Chinese history and his critical view of them. It's much freer with irregular lines (vs. the ridged five or seven words per line of the old Chinese poetry). It's charged with anger but also with humor, collaged with different texts—remarks from Mei Jinzhuang and other people and his own ripostes. By today's standards, it may

be seen as hybrid writing with some poetry and some prose (as po-
etry can only be lyrical and/or narrative but not a debate or an ar-
gument, which belongs to essays, according to the old definition.)
He even put footnotes directly into the poem by using parentheses,
which looks exciting today.

In November 2013, I wrote an essay to correct my previous com-
ments on Hu Shi and called for a "Reevaluation of Hu Shi." Chen
Jun 陈均 (1974–), a poet and poetry critic in Beijing, responded with
an essay in the same month saying that though it might be a fresh
look into the history, this poem was previously used as "background
materials" only, not as a poem. He tried to support me by saying that
this poem could be seen as doggerel (打油诗) and Hu Shi's *Book of
Experiments* contained some other doggerel poems, and other prom-
inent poets in the 1920s and 1930s of China also wrote doggerels.
I would like to argue that doggerels in Chinese history are usually
short and funny, but this poem is substantially long and serious, even
though it's funny at the same time.

Was Chinese New Poetry born in the U.S.?

Literally so. Hu Shi was in the US from 1910 to June 1917 with schol-
arships from the Boxer Indemnity Grant—first at Cornell studying
agriculture, but he changed to philosophy and literature and then
transferred to Columbia University to get his PhD in philosophy. It
was a time of great changes in China. The Qing Dynasty was over-
thrown in 1912, replaced by the Republic of China. The temporary
president Sun Yatsun was replaced by the first president of the coun-
try, Yuan Shikai, then Yuan died in 1916. Prior to that, World War I
broke out in 1914.

A new movement of poetry was taking place in Anglo-American
poetry that couldn't possibly escape Hu Shi's notice. He wrote "Eight
don'ts" and published them in the *New Youth* journal in October 1916
in Shanghai, with no response. He made it into an essay with a new

title, "A preliminary proposal for literary reform," and published it again in *New Youth* in January 1917, when the journal was relocated to Beijing, and this time he received an enormous response. Here is some of what he proposed then: Don't write things that say nothing; don't be sentimental; don't use clichés; don't avoid slangs or colloquial words. It may look similar to the Imagist manifestos, but he was studying Shakespeare, Tennyson, and Browning. His diaries show that he was also reading Chinese classical philosophy and literature and drawing strength from there.

"Reply to Old Mei", a revolutionary poem with lots of deep thoughts about a literary reform, has been buried in the author's diaries. I'm not even sure if it's politically correct to dig it out, a poem that was written in the US and not published in China. It's in vernacular Chinese and in the new form of free verse. If we take it as poetry, not only will the beginning of New Poetry be dated one year earlier, 1916, and Hu Shi's reputation will change a great deal, but also it will help us define what is New Poetry in China, and how it has evolved to what it is today. Hu Shi was proposing to create a modern Chinese through using it in poetry. Why poetry? Because vernacular language was already accepted in fiction writing, for instance it was used in the novel, *Water Margin: 108 Brothers*, in the Ming dynasty. Poetry would be his battle field to fight for a new language. "Reply to Old Mei" was in the new language and new form that he was promoting but why didn't he include it in his first poetry collection? I've found some clues in his diaries. Mei Jinzhuang (Old Mei), a literature major at Harvard at that time, laughed at this poem as "not a poem" "with no rhymes or refined language or craft at all." The other Chinese students laughed at it too: "It's a total failure." Hu Shi defended himself in the diaries: "It's a half-joking, half-serious experiment of verse in vernacular language. It might be worthless, but it's important in my personal history of writing . . . It's a satire."

"Reply to Old Mei" is informative and persuasive with historical views of the changes in Chinese language and literature. It has a kind of irony that's lacking in most of the poetry in the first five decades in New Poetry. It's carefully crafted with a balanced structure. It's direct, funny and dramatic. It's not sentimental—most of the poems in the 1920s of China were too sentimental and empty. Regarding Mei's accusation of no rhymes, I can see rhymes throughout the first stanza: *liang, chang, tang, zhang, dang, huang, kuang,* and throughout the second stanza: *xiao, diao, dao, yao, dao, niao, liao, nao, hao, diao, miao, jiao, mao, zao, bao, kao* and *hao,* although fewer in the rest of the poem. But who says free verse needs rhymes?

Does a poem need to be published to be a poem? If so, and if "Reply to Old Mei" is not considered a poem because it's not published, then what about the first two poems by his fellow poet Chen Hengzhe, which did get published in the *Overseas Students Quarterly* in 1916?

Chen Hengzhe 陈衡哲 (1890–1976) came to the US in 1914, first attending Vassar College, then University of Chicago. She returned to Beijing in 1920 and became the first woman scholar and professor in China. While in the US, she supported Hu Shi's literary reform by writing poems and short stories in the vernacular Chinese. In November 1916, she published two poems in the U.S. based *Overseas Students Quarterly*, and in May 1917, her first short story appeared in the same magazine. In 1918, she published more poems and short stories in the *New Youth* journal. Today, she is commonly considered as the first woman writer in Chinese modern history, arguably the first fiction writer even before the literary giant Lu Xun, who published his first short story in 1918, a year after hers. The question is whether literature published in diaspora magazines counts as part of the Chinese literary cannon. If publication anywhere in the world counts, she would be the first poet of Chinese New Poetry. But here comes, again, the question of what is New Poetry. I will reproduce her two poems below, along with my translations:

月

初月曳轻云，
笑隐寒林里；
不知好容光，
已映清溪底。

Moon

Thru' a thin cloud a new moon climbs up,
then fades out, a cold falling leaf;
but its radiant face reflected in the creek
stays in the clear water and won't leave.

风

夜闻雨敲窗，
起视月如水；
万叶正乱飞，
鸣飙落松蕊。

Wind

At night I hear the rain on my window.
I get up and see the moonlight, a waterfall.
Leaves fly around, soaring, and batter
the pine trees. The young cones fall.

On the surface level, she followed the traditional form of five-word quatrain with the typical -a-a one rhyme. Since Hu Shi never specified whether New Poetry should rhyme or not, plus there was a strong sentiment to stick to the rhyming systems, these two pieces could pass as New Poems. Hu Shi praised them and recorded them in his diaries, but he never took them as the first New Poetry, because he had published similar semi-new poems in the same diaspora magazine in 1914, especially the one titled "Big Snow." A true New Poem should be something like "Reply to Old Mei", without constraints of how many words in each line and how many lines in each stanza, or the tonal patterns (平仄) in each line and the "corresponding" (对仗) in each of the two lines. The Butterfly poem changed the usual line arrangement and the old rhyming pattern even though less free than the "Reply to Old Mei," with fewer variations. It was due to the vernacular Chinese used in the Butterfly poem, a language of daily conversational speech rather than the dead classical Chinese, that it was hailed as New Poetry. However, the Butterfly poem (dated August 23, 1916) was also written while he was in the US but somehow 1916 is not being considered as the year New Poetry started, except in this anthology.

What's new in New Poetry?

Confucius says "day by day make it new" (through Ezra Pound's translation); Hu Shi was experimenting with something new year by year. His literary experiment involved translation as well, using different types of Chinese from old to new. In 1914, he translated Browning's "Epilogue to Asolando" and Byron's "The Isles of Greece" in the ancient language style of Qu Yuan (343–278 BCE). Later in the same year, he visited Boston and Concord and translated Emerson, but this time in a much freer style:

> They reckon ill who leave me out;
>> When me they fly, I am the wings;
> I am the doubter and the doubt,
>> I am the hymn the Brahmin sings.

弃我者，其为计拙也。
背我而高飞者，不知我即其高飞之翼也。
疑我者，不知疑亦我也，疑我者亦我也。
其歌颂我者，不知其歌亦我也。

He called this "prose" but we call it free verse today. The language is classical sounding, but it suits this poem very well, tight and powerful. In July 1915, he wrote a poem in English about the Statue of Liberty in New York, with an implied reference to his literary reform in terms of ideas, language and form. "Crossing the Harbor" begins with, "As on the deck half-sheltered from the rain / We listen to the wintry wind's wild roars," and ends with, "And my comrade whispers to me, / There is 'Liberty'!" Except for a few words, it's a poem of free verse with the clear language that he was looking for in Chinese. I'm translating the whole poem into Chinese here:

《穿过港湾》

甲板上半遮挡着雨
我们听见冬天的风在狂野吼叫，
听见缓慢的波浪撞击大都会港岸；
我们搜寻地球之上
闪耀的群星
它们照亮了巨大黑暗的苍穹，——
在那里——
在那盛大的辐射球体之上，
一盏灯超群绝伦。
我的战友向我耳语，
看，那里有"自由"！

I often wonder why he didn't rewrite it in Chinese. It sounds contemporary. It seems that it was through writing free verse in English that he finally moved to the writing of Chinese free verse. In his later essays, he defined New Poetry as a new way of writing that started in the summer of 1915, born out of a long debate. So I would take all his writings in 1915 and 1916 as his experiments including his poems in English. Finally in July 1916, he wrote his loud declaration in that unpublished long poem in Chinese "Reply to Old Mei—A poem in plain speech."

Ezra Pound translated Chinese classical poetry into free verse in order to change English poetry. Hu Shi promoted New Poetry in order to change Chinese, to end the long separation of what's being spoken and what's being written, to push the birth of a modern Chinese, a living one like natural speech. His work was monumental like that of Dante.

Chen Hengzhe supported Hu Shi's reform by publishing two poems of the new language, but not in free verse. What she published later in 1918 was much less restricted—"People say I'm crazy 人家说我发了疯" was a dramatic monologue, with irregular lines, no rhymes, about an elderly patient rambling in a hospital. Influence from Robert Browning? Chinese ancient poets also used dramatic monologue. "River Merchant's Wife" by Li Bai (701–762) is an example. Was Robert Browning influenced by Chinese ancient poetry? Possibly. Especially since he spent much time in Italy. Marco Polo brought scrolls of poetry and painting to Italy. Later on, Tang poetry was introduced to Italy in the eighteenth century and became popular in Europe in the mid-nineteenth century. Browning had a Chinese friend who was a poet. But Li Bai's influence, if any, needs further research. Since the Chinese students enrolled in American colleges were also reading classical Chinese poetry and He Shi wrote classical poetry before coming to America, the apparent influence from Browning could be from the Tang poets.

Hu Shi won the Corson Browning Prize for his essay "A defense of Robert Browning's optimism." And among the many poets he translated into Chinese, such as Omar Khayyám, Goethe, Heine, Tennyson, Browning, Shelley, Byron, Campbell, Hardy, DH Lawrence, etc. he worked on Robert Browning more and with better efforts. The following is his Chinese translation with a very interesting syntax and rhythm:

> One who never turned his back but marched breast forward,
> Never doubted clouds would break,
> Never dreamed, though right were worsted, wrong would triumph,
> Held we fall to rise, are baffled to fight better,
> Sleep to wake.

(from "Epilogue" by Robert Browning)

> 从不转背而挺身向前，
> 从不怀疑云要破裂，
> 虽合理的弄糟，违理的战胜，
> 而从不作迷梦的，
> 相信我们沉而再升， 败而再战，
> 睡而再醒。

The following one is probably his best translation:

> Round the cape of a sudden came the sea,
> And the sun looked over the mountain's rim:
> And straight was a path of gold for him,
> And the need of a world of men for me.

("Parting at morning" by Robert Browning)

刚转个湾，忽然眼前就是海了，
太阳光从山头射出去：
他呢，前面一片黄金的大路，
我呢，只剩一个空洞洞的世界了。

The Chinese language here is fresh even looked at today. I would probably only change three words if it were my translation. Here "the need of a world of men" predicted the situation in his final days, just as the "Butterflies" described his solitude in his early years,

IS THE NEW POETRY MOVEMENT A RENAISSANCE IN CHINA?

Hu Shi's interest in literary and cultural reform went beyond poetry. He only wrote three hundred poems in Chinese, and translated thirty poems and a collection of seventeen short stories into Chinese. *The Collected Works* by Hu Shi published in mainland China in 2003, consisting of forty-four volumes, were mostly essays and diaries. As New Poetry continued blooming through the 1930s and 1940s, many other poets were more productive and left volumes of New Poetry. Hu Shi is now remembered as a pioneer of New Poetry, never a major poet, due to his own poor judgment in selecting what to publish, or the severe attacks from his contemporaries on his more serious experiments, such as the long poem "Reply to Old Mei" and his translation of Byron's "The Isles of Greece." He was proud of the translation he did in 1919 of Sara Teasdale's "Over the Roof," which was talked about excessively in the studies of New Poetry for the wrong reasons. He himself felt that he discovered a way of translating the iambic into Chinese, which further supported the use of modern Chinese: in classical Chinese each word is one syllable, but in modern vernacular Chinese one word can be two to three syllables, creating the stressed and unstressed. By imitating the English iambic lines, he created a new kind of free verse in Chinese. However, his translation of "Auld Robin Gray" (老洛伯), by the Scottish poet Anne Lindsay, flows better and has a more natural rhythm, and it's one of the best free verse poems in the early Chinese New Poetry.

To paraphrase what Hu Shi wrote in his diaries: his revolution was nothing really new—Dante wrote in Italian instead of Latin, Chaucer dispensed with old English, and Martin Luther moved from Latin into the German vernacular. As for the literary revolutions in China: Qu Yuan's poetry was the first revolution, short poems of five or seven words per line were the second revolution, the prose poems of the Han Dynasty (202–220) were the third, the regulated poetry of the Tang Dynasty (618–907) with a strict tonal system was the fourth, the deregulated Ci of Song Dynasty (920–1279) was the fifth, and the change from Ci to the lyrics and drama of Yuan (1271–1368) and Ming (1368–1644) Dynasties was the sixth revolution. He was merely continuing the spirit of making changes and moving forward.

If we look at the notorious Butterfly poem (两只黄蝴蝶) more closely, we will see that it's a double five-word quatrain (双绝句):

        xxxxx, xxxxx。 a
        xxxxx, xxxxx。 b
        xxxxx, xxxxx。 a
        xxxxx, xxxxx。 b

The regulated five-word quatrains in the High Tang Dynasty are five words per line and four lines per stanza, followed by an optional second stanza. The change to the double quatrains horizontally may look trivial, but the extended lines demonstrate the major changes in the language: in modern Chinese a word can be two to three characters, and therefore the new language doesn't fit into the old forms any more. (Also of note is that Hu Shi was the first to use punctuations in Chinese.) More importantly, he revived the old quatrain from the Tang Dynasty and gave it a new shape, the doubled lines. But why does it sound like a nursery rhyme today? Classical Chinese is elegant and refined but the language used in the Butterfly poem is vernacular Chinese which should be completely free like the way it's spoken or like "natural breathing."

Hu Shi acknowledged the vernacular language used in ancient poetry. As poetry died out in the Ming and Qing Dynasties, he called for a revival of poetry and revival of vernacular language. Vernacular Chinese has existed throughout history. Li Bai's best known poem, "Quiet night thought" was an example. Li Bai wrote two kinds of poetry, using either classical or vernacular Chinese. Hu Shi's literary reform was not a total break from tradition but also a call for a look back into ancient times for a renewed living language as he rediscovered the vernacular poetry in the Tang Dynasty by Wang Fanzhi and Han Shan (Cold Mountain) who later became widely known in America through translations by Gary Snyder and Burton Watson.

Li Shutong 李叔同 (1880–1942), Hu Shi's contemporary, eleven years older than him, spent five years in Japan studying art and music and returned to China in 1910, the year Hu Shi left China for the US. Li and several others brought Western culture to China through Japan, and Li was the first to teach Western painting and music in China. In 1915, he wrote the lyrics for a song, "Farewell," breaking the traditional metrical system of poetry. It was rediscovered in the 1940s and again in the 1980s.

Farewell

Outside the pavilion, along the ancient trail
green grass stretches joining the horizon.
Evening wind blows willows, a faded flute
while the sun sets over mountains and mountains.
At the sky's end, and the ocean's corner,
friends are scattered with only a few to hold.
Tonight we drink and exhaust the joy,
then we'll part and our dreams turn cold.

The original Chinese has alternating numbers of characters/space in each line, with an incredibly amazing pause in the first line of each stanza:

```
xxx, xxx    (a)
xxxxx       (a)
xxxxxxx     (b)
xxxxx       (b)

xxx, xxx    (c)
xxxxx       (c)
xxxxxxx     (b)
xxxxx       (b)
```

It's rhymed but not in the traditional way. The language is simple and plain, a little bit melancholy, awaking a sense of nostalgia immediately. It's not cutting edge by today's standards, but it was innovative in 1915. The lyric was written under the influence of a Japanese lyricist who re-wrote the lyrics for an American song, but each was independent work. I would love to take this as the first New Poem in Chinese history. However, Li Shutong didn't have a manifesto of literary reform or the consciousness of nationwide reform expressed elsewhere, such as in essays. Nor did he influence anyone. The other consideration is: to discuss literary influence from Japan is not politically correct in China, because of the Japanese invasion of China in the 1930s and because of national pride. It might be for the same reason that Hu Shi's poetry, written in the US and unpublished in China, is never considered as Chinese poetry. Or perhaps I'm oversensitive. It might well be that most poets have not seen "Reply to Old Mei." Personally, I'm not really concerned about where New Poetry was born but how it has evolved. Li Shutong in China and Hu Shi in America were both trying to write a new kind of poetry using plain spoken language through "living words" with some ancient elements. It has been noted that Li Shutong's "Farewell" poem resembles the poetic style of Fan Zhongyan (989–1052) in the Song Dynasty, which supports the notion that the New Poetry movement in the early 20th century was a Renaissance in its full meaning.

What's most important and mostly forgotten is that New Poetry is not opposed to the ancient poetry in China, but rather to the classical language (文言文), especially the "eight-legged" language (八股文) that prevailed in the Qing Dynasty (1644–1912), which was becoming more and more rigid and stiff because of the long Imperial Examination System (科举制) from 605 to 1905. The ending of that system and the downfall of the Qing Dynasty made the literary reform possible. As Hu Shi indicated, New Poetry was a renaissance of ancient Chinese poetry, using plain and clear language for a complicated modern life.

Hu Shi was also interested in earlier poetry from the Middle East. He translated Omar Khayyám (1046–1131) so beautifully:

> 要是天公换了卿和我,
> 该把这糊涂世界一齐打破,
> 再磨再炼再调和,
> 好依着你我的安排, 把世界重新造过!

—Rubaiyat #73

It's interesting to notice that the Rubaiyat (鲁拜集) has the same shape as the Tang quatrains, four lines per stanza, and the same rhyming patterns. But what's new in Hu Shi's Chinese translation is a music made possible by using modern Chinese with a classical tone. As "Reply to Old Mei" says, "Texts of three thousand years, up and down, living or dead, / who knows how many have been hijacked." In a positive sense, being "hijacked" can bring changes, something ancient with a new life.

Artistically, "Reply to Old Mei" is quite contemporary with its hybrid writing and collage of various types of texts. It's the traditional standard view of what is poetry that makes it a nonpoetry piece. I'm even beginning to wonder if *The Book of Songs* edited by Confucius was really the first anthology of poetry in Chinese history. We have *The Book of Mountains and Seas* (山海经) from the ancient times, an epic of eighteen volumes about the mythologies, geographies, and polytheistic religions of ancient China. Why has it never been considered as poetry? Is it because of its irregular shape (a different number of words in each line) and lack of rhymes? What else was filtered by Confucius? According to his standard, "Reply to Old Mei" would never be a poem, ever, despite the fact that there has never been any other writing, not to say poetry, that has defended poetry in contemporary China more powerfully and eloquently in the entire past one hundred years.

Ming Di
January 2016
Los Angeles and Beijing

Acknowledgments

Chen Jun's two poems first appeared in *Poetry* (translated by MD). Yu Xiuhua's two poems first appeared in *World Literature Today* (tr. by MD). Lü De'an's poem "Night at Ocean Corner, and Women" first appeared in *Gulf Coast* (tr. by MD). Liu Xia's "Road to Darkness" and Liu Xiaobo's "Morning" first appeared in the *New York Review of Books* (tr. by MD). "For My Daughter" by Liao Yiwu previously appeared in *Tupelo Quarterly* (tr. by MD). "Fragment No. 8" by Liu Xia was first published by *PEN America*, then included in *Empty Chairs*: *Poems* by Liu Xia (tr. by Ming Di and Jennifer Stern, Graywolf Press, 2015). "Flying Association" by Zang Di first appeared in an earlier version in *The Book of Cranes*: *Poems* by Zang Di (translated by Ming Di and Neil Aitken, Vagabond Press, 2015). "Mirror" By Zhang Zao was first published by *Poetry International/Rotterdam*. Poems of Chen Dongdong, Li Yawei, Pan Xichen, Song Wei, Mo Mo, Qiu Huadong, Ni Zhijuan, Jiang Hao, Xuanyuan Shike, Qin Sanshu, and Su Xiaoyan translated by MD first appeared in "Letters from Beijing" published on the website of Poetry International/SDSU. Appreciation and gratitude to all the editors of the above mentioned journals and publishers.

Of the 136 poems selected here, ten first appeared in their earlier versions in *New Cathay: Contemporary Chinese Poetry* (ed. MD, Tupelo Press, 2013): "To Xuefei" by Zhang Shuguang (tr. by Katie Farris and Ming Di), "Nothing to do with Crows" by Sun Wenbo (tr. by MD and Neal Aitken), "Diary" by Wang Jiaxin (tr. by MD), "Rhetoric" by Liao Yiwu (tr. by KF and MD), "Mao Zedong" by Xiao Kaiyu (tr. by MD and NA), "The Clay Pot in Tennessee" by Yang Xiaobin (tr. by MD and NA), "A Homebound Guy" by Jiang Tao (tr. by MD, NA and TB), "Poetry Doesn't Know It's Dead" by Lü Yue (tr. by MD and NA), "Mama Ana Paula Also Writes Poetry" by Hu Xudong (tr by KF and

MD), and "Geometry" by Jiang Li (tr by MD and NA). The editor is forever grateful to Tupelo Press.

Work from the Translation Workshops at Beijing Normal University organized by Zhang Qinghua and Ming Di:

Gregory Pardlo (GP) with Henry Zhang:
  Zhang Qinghua
Gregory Pardlo (GP) with Hao Wang:
  Li Sen
Kevin Young (KY) with Henry Zhang:
  Ouyang Jianghe
  Hu Xian
Tracy K. Smith (TKS) with Changtai Bi:
  Yi Lei (two poems)
Michelle Chihara (MC) and Tony Barnstone (TB):
  Zhou Qingrong
Rachel Galvin (RG) and Ming Di (MD):
  Tong Wei

Poems from the *Poetry East West* journal (ed. MD):

George Szirtes (GS):
  Yang Lian
Fiona Sze-Lorrain (FSL):
  Bai Hua
Dian Li (DL) and Kerry Shawn Keys (KSK):
  Song Lin
Neil Aitken (NA) and Ming Di (MD):
  Qin Xiaoyu
Tony Barnstone (TB) and Ming Di (MD):
  Leng Shuang

Jidi Majia

Tremendous appreciation to all of the above poet-translators.

108 poems specifically translated for this anthology:

Translated by Ming Di (MD):
Wen Yiduo, Fei Ming, Feng Zhi, Dai Wangshu, Bian Zhilin,
Ji Xian, Zhu Yingdan, Wu Xinghua, Lü Yuan, Huang Xiang,
Luo Qing, Bei Dao, Duo Duo (3), Liu Xiaobo, Lü De'an (2),
Mo Fei, Chen Dongdong, Luo Yihe, Zhang Zao, Qing Ping,
Wang Yin, Xi Chuan (2), Li Yuansheng, Zang Di, Zhao Ye,
Na Ye (2), Pan Wei, Xiao Xiao, Shen Wei, Lei Pingyang, Gu Ma,
Chi Lingyun (2), Yu Nu, Chen Xianfa, Sang Ke, Lan Lan,
Lin Zi, Huang Bin, Qiu huadong, Yu Xiang, Ni Zhijuan,
Jiang Hao, Han Bo, Chen Jun (2), Mu Cao, Shen Haobo (2),
Yu Xiuhua (2), Zheng Xiaoqiong, Xiao Shui, Yuan Yongping,
Jike Bu, Xu Lizhi, Qin Sanshu, Su Xiaoyan (63 poems)

Translated by Ming Di (MD) and Kerry Shawn Keys (KSK):
Hu Shi, Li Jinfa, Chen Jingrong, Mu Dan, Zheng Min,
Luo Fu, Guan Guan, Shang Qin, Zheng Chouyu, Chang Yao,
Liang Bingjun, Mang Ke, Gen Zi, Yan Li, Yu Jian (2),
Wang Xiaoni, Zhai Yongming, Mo Yan, Han Dong, Sen Zi,
Li Yawei, Pan Xichen, Hai Zi, Song Wei (2), Mo Mo,
Zhang Zhihao, Shu Cai, Yu Xiaozhong, Yi Sha, Xi Du (2),
Li Shaojun, Jing Wendong, Zhu Zhu, An Qi, Xi Wa,
Xuanyuan Shike, Quan Zi, Zhang Er, Li Hongwei, Ma Yan,
Li Heng, Kawa Niangji (45 poems)